PRESENCE and ABSENCE

*Studies in Phenomenology and
Existential Philosophy*

GENERAL EDITOR

James M. Edie

CONSULTING EDITORS

PRESENCE

A Philosophical Investigation

and ABSENCE

of Language and Being

ROBERT SOKOLOWSKI

Indiana University Press

BLOOMINGTON & LONDON

Copyright © *1978 by Robert Sokolowski*

All rights reserved

MANUFACTURED IN THE UNITED STATES OF AMERICA

Library of Congress Cataloging in Publication Data

Sokolowski, Robert.
    Presence and absence.

    (Studies in phenomenology and existential philosophy)
    Includes index.
    1. Knowledge, Theory of. 2. Analysis (Philosophy) 3. Phenomenology. 4. Ontology.
I. Title.
BD241.S63 1978   121   77-23628 L . C
ISBN 0-253-34600-2 1 2 3 4 5 82 81 80 79 78

To My Parents

Sapienter ac sine confusione dicitur: 'Nix alba est,' quia verum est. Non autem minus verum est, mentiri eum qui dicit: 'Nix nigra est.' Non minus ergo sapienter et inconfusibiliter dicitur: 'Si enim recipis hoc quia verum est, nulli vero contradicas amplius.' Si enim placet hoc pomum quia dulce est, cur non omnia eundem habentia saporem, similiter placeant?

–*Meditationes Guigonis Prioris Cartusiae, n.* 155.*

"With wisdom and without confusion do we say, 'Snow is white,' because it is true. It is no less true that anyone who says, 'Snow is black,' tells a lie. Therefore we must go on to say, no less wisely and no less clear of confusion: 'If you accept this because it is true, you should never in the future contradict anything that is true.' For if this fruit delights you because it is sweet, why should not everything that has the same flavor please you in the same way?"

–*Meditations of Guigo, Prior of the Charterhouse, n.* 155.

*Le Recueil des Pensées du B. Guigue, ed. Dom André Wilmart, O.S.B. (Paris: Librairie philosophique J. Vrin, 1936).

CONTENTS

ACKNOWLEDGMENTS

I wish to express my indebtedness and my gratitude to Thomas Prufer for his help in both the substance and the details of this book. I am also grateful to Eileen Powers for her generous and cordial assistance in typing the manuscript.

Some elements in chapter eleven of this book were presented as a paper entitled "The Presence of Judgment" at the 1974 meeting of the *Deutsch Gesellschaft für phänomenologische Forschung* in Berlin; the paper was published in *Phänomenologische Forschungen*, 2 (1976), pp. 19-28. An earlier version of some materials in chapters nine and ten was delivered under the title "The Ideal Existence of Judgments" at the 1976 meeting of the same society in Munich; it was published in *Phänomenologische Forschungen*, 4 (1977), pp. 86-102.

Passages from Plato are given in the Jowett translation. The quotation from Ezra Pound's Canto xlv, from *The Cantos (1-95)*, copyright © 1938 by Ezra Pound and published by New Directions Publishing Co. and Faber and Faber Ltd., is gratefully acknowledged.

Introduction

We can use words and entertain things thoughtlessly, or we can mind what we say and what we experience. We are familiar with the difference between being thoughtful and being thoughtless, but to be familiar with the difference is not yet to think about it. Part of the work of philosophy is to say what thoughtfulness is: we are encouraged not simply to put our minds to what we say and encounter, but to explain what "minding" is. And once we begin to ask about thoughtfulness, we are led inevitably to ask about the truthfulness of things which permits thinking to come about. Thinking is not something we do entirely on our own; we are allowed to think by what our thoughts are about. Thus when philosophy tries to think about thinking, it must also talk about what solicits thinking and permits it to occur. The name for what solicits thinking and permits it to occur is "being," and our attempt to discuss thinking will gradually move, in the final chapters of this book, into the question of being. Our analyses of the components of thinking and truthfulness—naming, referring, registering, grammar, the sentence and the proposition, the essential and the coincidental—remain provisional until the final contexts of being are examined in the last two chapters. In addition, our study of thinking must also examine the thoughtlessness and the obscurity out of which thinking emerges.

If we are to do justice to thinking and to truthfulness, our analysis must use elements that are appropriate. The appropriate elements for the analysis of thinking and truthfulness are presence, absence, and the interplay between the two. Only by moving into these dimensions can we understand what things like names or phonemes or propositions, and all the other "parts" of thinking and truthfulness, are. The use of the play of presence and absence provides us, for example, with a fundamental explanation of what naming is, and once we have acquired this explanation we can go on to compare names with predicates, concepts, signs, definite descriptions, or other "parts" of thinking; but if we have not yet shown how naming achieves presences and controls absences, comparisons of names with other elements in language and thought remain superficial and fail to come to terms with what they desire to explain. Naming involves one form of the play of presence and absence; the achievement of phonemes involves another form of it; another is at work in perception and in prepredicative experience, and still another in distinguishing propositions from facts. By showing how presence and absence work in these and in other elements of thinking and truthfulness, we give a philosophical account of such elements and hence come to understand what they are.

My use of the play of presence and absence is derived from Husserl, who formulates it as the synthesis of empty and filled intentions. The theme of the empty and the filled, and of the identity that is achieved through this couple, is the predominant concern of Husserl's philosophy. He not only describes how presence and absence work in the various fields of our experience, but also explains how we are able to reflect philosophically upon presence and absence. Husserl's writings have not yet yielded all that they promise, and I hope that this book may indicate what might be done with them. Because Husserl's thought provides elements of definition that have not been used in other philosophical traditions, some terms defined in this book may acquire senses that are somewhat different from the meanings they have in the work of other philosophers. For example, in chapter one "reference" is defined partly by the presence of an addressee for our speech; the referential use of words is contrasted to what I call the evocative use, in which we remain alone—in the absence of addressees—while using words to think about things. This contrast between solitary and public speech makes explicit as a theme the presence or absence of an addressee and shows the effect his presence has on the syntactical element in what we say. In chapter one we explore an array of distinctions that can be made in the use of words when we take into account the presence and absence of an addressee, and also the presence and absence of what is being discussed; this is an initial exercise in some contrasts of presence and absence, a prelude to the more complex differentiations in the chapters that follow.

Chapters two to ten are a phenomenology of thought and language which ranges from the level of sounds and phonemes, through words and sentences, to an analysis of the proposition. In chapter two we show how the grammatical structure of nouns and verbs in sentences is related to the awareness that there can be contexts distinct from the context in which the sentence is being spoken; this awareness of absent contexts marks a development beyond the more primitive consciousness, expressed in a "gerundial" form of speech, which sees everything as simply continuous with one's immediate surroundings. Chapters three and four examine how naming is constituted by the play of presence and absence, and how other indicating sounds and terms, such as cries, exclamations, demonstratives, and the definite article, can also be described in function of what is present or not present to whoever makes the sounds or expresses the terms. The origins of syntax in prepredicative experience, which includes the activity of "taking" something "as" something or other, are examined in chapter five, and the complications of syntax are treated in chapter six. These complications are contrasted, in the same chapter, to the procedure of turning a fact into a proposition; following Husserl, I define a proposition as a fact taken as proposed or supposed by someone.

The proposition so defined is then examined, in chapters seven to ten, in its relation to the sentence that expresses it, and in its very different relation to the perceptual activity that it can direct. The proposition is described as a special kind of rule that governs the sentence that expresses it, and the grammatical parts of sentences are described as signals of the propositional activity that goes on between speaker and addressee. The use of such categories as rule and signal emphasizes the fact that thinking, thoughtful speech, and thoughtful listening are activities, and these activities are all related to the activity of thoughtful perception, in which truth is accomplished as disclosure and not only as confirmation. In chapter ten, where these themes are brought to completion, the concepts of naming and expression are also further clarified. Chapter eleven consolidates our analyses by taking care of several details worthy of note, and chapter twelve turns to the difference between recognizing and failing to recognize the essentials of what we talk about. This chapter tries to show how "essences" are at work in our thinking and experience. In contrast to the concerns with syntax and the formal elements of language that predominate in the book so far, the concern with essentials and coincidentals is involved with the content or the kinds of things we discuss and know. Finally the last three chapters of the book examine philosophical speech and thought. Chapter thirteen describes philosophy as the exploration of the various plays of presence and absence that can take place; we here give an account of the kinds of analyses that were carried on throughout the previous chapters of the book. Chapter fourteen describes first philosophy as the study of being as being and explains how this is more than an analysis of presence and absence; and chapter fifteen asks what kind of thinking is still available beyond philosophy and first philosophy.

As some references will indicate, many of the Husserlian themes used in the book figure prominently in the early lectures of Martin Heidegger, which are now being published in his collected works. Husserl has also influenced the work of Roman Jakobson, and the references in this book to Jakobson are meant to point the way to further use of phenomenology in the structural analysis of language. In the final chapters of the book, the attempt to discuss the question of being and to explore thinking beyond philosophy involves, as one would expect, a greater use of Heidegger and a diminished reference to Husserl; it also allows us to situate the linguistic and phenomenological issues of the book's earlier chapters within the philosophical concerns of Plato and Aristotle.

PRESENCE and ABSENCE

CHAPTER 1

Five Ways of Naming Things

To be a name normally involves being a sound. If we wish to understand names philosophically, we must contrast them not to silence but to sounds that fail to be names and yet are usually uttered in the presence of certain objects. I may, for example, become accustomed to making a certain sound when a particular object, or a particular kind of object, appears: something red appears and I cry "red"; it starts to snow and I call out "snow" or "white" or some other sound; a familiar person arrives and I react with "daddy." Such reactions may arise because I imitate others who have repeatedly made them when the object in question is around, or they might be devices I get used to using on my own; I contribute to a similar context by similar behavior. My reaction is solicited by the associative pull of what is presented to me. My vocal responses are not very much different from any other response I might make to things which appear alike; instead of making sounds I might make certain gestures, salivate, or become frightened.

The same vocal reaction may occur when the object is absent in certain ways. I may make these sounds while I am daydreaming about the object, or when I get some hints, like noises or odors associated with it, that it is somewhere in the vicinity. The object may be only marginally or only imaginatively present and still provoke the sound. Or, in a more thorough kind of absence, I may urgently feel the need for the object and use the sound as an attempt to call it to me: "water" may be uttered not as a name but as a combined appeal and groan. The sound is still pulled by association, but the association arises from a felt need, not from a sensed presence. The sound rounds out, by association with what I have experienced in the past, the thirst I now feel. Although the object is absent, and is felt as absent, this absence is not the kind that turns a vocal utterance into a name.

A vocal response can become a name when I not only have the object before me, but appreciate it as present. I recognize that the object here does not have to be here; it could have been absent instead. I appreciate its presence as contrasted to its absence. I not only enjoy the object, I enjoy the object as present. Then I can name it; I am no longer limited to making a voiced response to it. I am said to have acquired some distance toward the object. But the distance in question is not spatial, it involves only the intrusion of the "as present" between the object and me. This is what makes the object nameable.

I now can "have" the object in mind as something to be spoken about; I no longer merely have it to be consumed, fondled, or provoked. Things can be said about an object only when it is so held by a name. This holding by name does not, of course, damage or improve or change the object; it does not tamper with it in any way that might make us say anything different about it, in ordinary or in scientific discourse, than we would have said apart from its being held by us. The object being named and discussed is not chemically or physically affected. Still, a certain excellence is realized in the object when it is named and discussed, if "being known" is to be considered a kind of perfection in it. But this is a perfection examined by philosophy, not by our nonphilosophical attempts to find out facts and laws about the object in question.

Philosophically we cannot understand what names are unless we pay attention to the difference between holding something and holding something as present. A being that uses a name does not just have an object, it has the object as present. As philosophers we contemplate the user of names and try to describe what makes it possible for him to name things. We as philosophers do not introduce names, nor do we introduce the elements—the difference between an object and an object as present—that make naming possible; this is all done before philosophy. Philosophy, therefore, is parasitic on what is achieved before it begins its exploration. However, we can make thematic what the user of names takes for granted. He must have recognized the object as present, since he has named it, but he may not be able to say that the "as present" is what makes his naming possible. To say this, and to elaborate what it means, is a clarification which only philosophy can achieve.

We will return to the establishment of names in chapter three. At present we must examine different ways in which names can be used, and we begin by distinguishing two, the evocative and the referential. A name is used referentially when we speak to someone else about the thing named; our words bring his mind to the object. A name is used evocatively when we refrain from addressing someone else, when we let the name simply hold the object in focus for our own exploration. In evocation we invite the named object to suggest its appropriate words, and so become truthful, in us, but we do not speak to anyone. The distinction between the referential and the evocative depends on whether or not we involve someone besides ourselves as an audience in our use of names.

When we use names referentially we must take into account not only the object we speak about but also the person to whom we speak. Our selection of names and our choice of the additional words needed to compose whole sentences must be made not only because of what we see in the object, but also in deference to our interlocutor: what words are best to make our statement clear to him? There is a rhetorical dimension to words used in reference. Thus in the evocative use of names there are only three elements: the speaker, the object, and words; but in the referential use there are four: the speaker, the object, words, and the addressee. When these elements are mixed in different ways, different effects on the names and syntax of sentences are produced. In particular, the following four possibilities must be distinguished.

(1) In the evocative use of names, the composition, the putting-together of words, is of minimal importance. We do not speak explicitly to ourselves, and whether I organize whole, distinct sentences does not matter much. The center of focus is the object. The words help me hold the object in view and help me notice aspects and arrangements in it, but their function is to assist perception, not to make an explicit statement. The words function with

the imprecision of perception itself: "cup-white-floral-orange"; such words may emerge inchoately to help me explore the thing, but I do not yet publicly assert anything about it, though I may be getting ready to do so. Because they do not make up an explicit statement, you, the reader, may not be sure what I mean by the four words inside the quotation marks, although they would have served adequately enough when I used them privately.

Besides failing to be assembled into distinct sentences, the words themselves may be imperfectly formed and may be used with idiosyncratic meanings, metaphorically, or as mere suggestions. They are subordinated to the perception. Of course the names we learn in our inherited language will urge us to notice certain aspects in the object, but they do not predestine us to see only these; words compel only those persons who cannot resist an urge. It is always possible to break through the pressure of language and notice aspects that others may not see, aspects that have not yet been institutionalized in the language. Indeed, it is the very indeterminacy of words in their evocative use which makes it impossible for them to coerce us into seeing only what they normally name.

(2) Once I begin to refer to the object in the company of an interlocutor, I have to be more decisive. I have to make a statement: "This cup has an orange floral design." The linkage of my words has to be more deliberately chosen. The words intrude more forcefully. Still, if my interlocutor and I are speaking about something we both perceive, the words remain very much subordinated to the object, and elliptical constructions can be accepted with no ambiguity in meaning: "He's angry; his gestures; expression; the eyes; calming down a bit now." The syntax can fade away. However, each word, each linguistic unit, has to be well formed and identifiable for the benefit of the interlocutor; in my solitary evocative use of language, the hint of a word suffices to assist my perception.

(3) The reason elliptical sentences suffice in the previous case is that my addressee and I have the object in view, and what is going on in it ought to be obvious to us. My words are added to coax his perceptions along lines I want him to follow, but the grooves are laid in the way the object appears; my words only give an assist. But we can also refer to an object which is not in our perceptual presence. Then my words become much more dominant and the

sentential construction, the grammar or syntax, cannot be neglected. Assertions or claims are then made about things that are not around to be seen, and I must be clear about what kind of claim I am making; the object is not there to take up the slack.

Let us stipulate that "reporting" means making statements about an object which is absent from our perception, and "registration" means making them about an object which is perceptually present. When I report, my addressee and I continue to think about the object which is absent. I use names to refer to that object; I name the absent. But because the object is not there to absorb our attention, and because I have to be more precise about what I am stating, I put my sentences together with greater care. I am also more concerned with the rhetorical aspect of my speech and try to select words and constructions that are appropriate for my interlocutor. I may even wish to embellish my sentences for the sheer pleasure of doing so. It would not be fitting for me to do this while I was registering certain facts about an object; if I began decorating my sentences then, I would, in effect, interrupt our common perception of the object and draw attention to my speech.

(4) Words and sentences begin to predominate when we go from registration to reporting. Still greater attention is drawn to words when we move from speaking to writing or reading. The words now attract the eye as well as the ear; they engage our sensibility more thoroughly than they do in reporting and registration. Furthermore, our sentences can become still more elaborate: the restrictions that speaking out loud puts on complexity and length are removed; the rhythm and limits of breath-groups become less important; our inability to hold very much in mind can be neglected; structure wins out over the substrate of sound which it forms, and can now stretch into sinuosities and involvements which would be impossible in speech. But although the written word is less transparent than the spoken, it never becomes entirely opaque: even in writing, names still refer. We still think about the object when we read, unless the intricacy or beauty of the writing, or the remarkable character of the script, makes us turn entirely to what is written.

Reading brings us back to something like the solitude we discussed in the evocative use of names, because we no longer involve the direct accompaniment of someone else. But the need to read, perceptually, makes it impossible for us to perceive the object we are reading about, except in the form of a marginal imagination; this is why it is so hard to learn to make certain identifications through books, such as learning to recognize musical structures, or flowers, or birds; we learn these things best when others point them out to us. Furthermore, the intricacy of written sentences is at the opposite extreme from the fragments of language which accompany our perception of things. Finally, reading differs from evocation because it involves a kind of interlocutor, someone who composed the text, whereas we are alone with language in evocation. However, despite these differences between reading and the evocative use of words, we cannot say that reading is a simple case of the referential use of names either. Reading falls between evocation and reference, and clarifying how it does so will help us understand, philosophically, the nature of both reading and writing.

A speaker intervenes actively and immediately in the second and third cases we have examined, in the articulation of a perceived object and in reporting. In these two cases, the speaker is much more prominent when he reports than when he assists perception. When he verbally articulates a shared perception, he does not go out on a limb; he simply displays what others can also see. His intelligence may be required to make the display, and the appearance articulated might not have been possible without him, but he only shows what can become evident to all. In reporting, however, the evidence is not at hand and we have to trust the speaker. He more explicitly takes a position, which then can be attributed to him. He emerges more conspicuously as the one responsible for a certain claim. When he articulates a perception his responsibility is subordinated to what almost anyone can see in the object; he merely helps us see it. But when he informs us about a fact, he does more than help: he gives us the opinion, and we receive it from him, not from the object.

The case in which a speaker articulates a perceived object can be further divided into two kinds. If he simply cajoles the perception of his interlocutor, he need not construct his sentences completely. Snatches of words suffice: "he's coming back now, looking around, surprised. . . ." Little more than this is done, for example, by commentators of sports on television (whereas radio commentators must take on the responsibility of reporting). This kind of commentary is sufficient when the listener is quite capable of articulating the object himself, with only a small assist. But if he is rather helpless to interpret what is going on, the speaker will have to be more explicit and tell him the facts before him. In this case the speaker assumes a greater responsibility; he almost—but not quite—begins to report, to become the sole source of information for the interlocutor. But he does not become a reporter, because the listener has the object before him and can see for himself, even if he can barely figure out what is happening. And when the speaker tells the other person what is going on, he has to frame well-formed sentences. Just as in reporting, ellipses and snatches of words are not enough. The speaker has to take a definite position and state distinctly what he is trying to say, and the grammatical or syntactical dimension of speech becomes paramount in such an explicit statement. The syntax of speech is an issue when we take a definite position and become responsible for what we say; it is less important when our words merely limn a perception.

With our new subdivision, the four cases we earlier distinguished become five:

1. evocation;
2. helping articulate a shared perception;
3. taking over and telling someone what is going on;
4. reporting;
5. writing and reading.

Although reporting is confined to one of the five positions in this series, registration ranges over the first three; it obviously is found in the second and third cases, but it also occurs in evocation, when we, although alone, explicitly begin to think about what is going on before us. Also, as we have observed, the syntactical element of speech becomes more prominent as we move from the first to the fifth of these ways of using language. And although evocation is mentioned first, it is obviously not the first use of language we learn; individual and internal speech can come only after we have been involved with other speakers in the second, third, and fourth ways of naming and speaking.[1]

Let us define syntax as the aspect of speech concerned with the linkage of words into sentences. It can appear in word order, inflexion, and in auxiliary words. It is to be contrasted to what we will call "lexicon," the aspect of words concerned with naming things. As we define them, syntax and lexicon are not two kinds of words: they are two aspects of words, and most words will have both a syntactical and a lexical dimension. "Lamppost" obviously names and so is lexical, but it is also a noun and hence has a syntactical aspect too. Some words may seem to be sheer syntactical units, like "nevertheless" or the "has" in "he has come," and we will examine whether any words are sheer names; but usually the word has both dimensions. At times we will use "grammar" as a synonym for syntax; and later in the book, when we distinguish between propositions and sentences, we will have to distinguish between sentential syntax and propositional syntax. However, our understanding of propositions is such that there may be considerable overlap between the sentential and the propositional, so the use of the single word "syntax" for both domains will not prove to be out of order.

Syntax becomes prominent in reporting and in explicitly telling others what is happening before them; for this a well-rounded whole of language, a well-linked sentence is necessary. Syntax is less important when our words merely accentuate a perception, whether for someone else or, in the evocative use of words, for ourselves alone. Here the lexical or naming dimension predominates, and even words which normally enjoy a syntactical dimension may allow it to fade into indifference. The syntax, which has to be well rounded and whole in reporting and informing, may in writing go farther and become enormously complex, enjoying intricacies which could not be attempted in speaking.

A linguistic whole, a sentence or a larger discourse with an identifiable beginning and end, is said to be consistent if it is properly put together. It does not contradict, does not "speak against" itself. An inconsistent speech is one in which a certain move is made in the linkage, along with another move that annuls the first. Consistency and inconsistency are matters of syntax. But the lexicon can be well or badly put together also, and then the linguistic whole is said to be coherent or incoherent. An incoherent speech does not cancel itself, as an inconsistent one does, but it tries to put together things that do not blend with one another (provided the names are being taken literally). The words resist one another in this union, whereas in inconsistency they annihilate each other. For example, "tall virtue sleeps furiously" is consistent syntactically but incoherent, because its lexical core, "virtue-tall-sleeps-furious," is made up of names that do not belong to one another, and they do not belong together because they could not serve to articulate a perception when they are assembled in this order.[2]

We have introduced the concept of naming as something contrasted to vocal utterances made in reaction to things, and we have distinguished five ways in which naming can occur, depending on whether we are alone or speaking to someone else, whether the object we speak about is present or absent to us, and whether we speak or read and write. Cutting across these possibilities are the distinctions between evocation and reference, and between the syntactical and the lexical aspects of words. All these distinctions occur within the horizon set by naming; only because objects appear as present are lexicon and syntax, evocation and reference, reporting and registration and the rest made possible. Moreover, all these distinctions—registration and reporting and the other ways of naming things—are not distinctions within any particular language, but are structural differences that arise because we speak with and to others, in both the presence and the absence of things, because we can either speak or read and write, and because we can withdraw from conversation and think about things by ourselves. They are differences in the activity of using language for the presencing of things.

Notes

1. On inner speech and the diminished function of syntax in it, see Lev Vygotsky, *Thought and Language*, trans. E. Hanfmann and G. Vakar (Cambridge: The M.I.T. Press, 1962), chapter 7.

2. On consistency and inconsistency, coherence and incoherence, see Edmund Husserl, *Formal and Transcendental Logic*, trans. D. Cairns (The Hague: Nijhoff, 1969), §14, §89, and Appendix I.

CHAPTER 2

Nouns, Verbs, and Contexts

The simplest kind of sentence appears to be made up of a noun and a verb. The noun, in its more elementary forms, names an individual, a group, or a class, while the verb either names an activity the subject is said to be engaged in, or it names a characteristic the subject is said to possess: John runs, men quarrel, Paul is short, cats are sly. But perhaps we can dig deeper into what the verb names. The verb can be considered as naming something more basic than, and therefore common to, both performing an action and having an attribute; it can be taken to name a manifestation. It names the way the subject appears. The "process" of appearing can occur either in an action performed by the subject or simply in the possession of an attribute.

The appearance named by the verb is not to be taken in a comparative sense; we do not mean the appearance as contrasted to the reality, what the subject just seems to be as opposed to what it truly is. Normally a thing is as it appears and its manifestation shows what it is. Exceptions to this, illusory or misleading appearances, are special cases. They can be recognized and explained only because they are deviations from what we normally find.

Because the verb names a manifestation, it always connotes a context. Something appears at a certain time and with a particular mixture of circumstances. This is why Aristotle claims that verbs differ from nouns by involving time in what they signify: not only do they name a way of appearing, they imply a time when this appearance takes place. Different languages may, of course, articulate this connotation of time in very different fashion; present, past, and future tenses are only one way of doing it. Some languages, for example, may express whether the process is completed or continuing, and this too is a temporal difference related to the situation in which the sentence is uttered. Nouns, however, when considered in their primary function as the subjects of sentences, move away from a definite context. They name something that can appear in another way in another context at another time. Underneath the various grammatical peculiarities of different languages, therefore, we find "the nominal element in the sentence, which names something that might enter into other sentences under other circumstances, and a phenomenal element proper to the particular occasion and never precisely to be repeated."[1]

The pull of nouns away from a definite situation occurs in different degrees. A proper name like "Konrad Adenauer" can be used to name its designate in various circumstances during the course of his life, but it could not name him as the subject of appearances, actual or possible, outside the span of a century or so. The common noun "elephant" can apply only in contexts during which biological and climatic conditions permit the existence of such beasts, although within that broad setting there are innumerable situations, generic and particular, actual and possible, in which the elephant does something or has a certain attribute and can serve as the named subject of a sentence. Names of material elements seem to pull farthest from any context. Sulfur might appear on our earth, on other bodies in the solar system, and in any galaxy. The context for such objects seems to be the entire universe.

However, part of the context of being named is the presence of someone who does the naming; things cannot manifest themselves except to a receiver, a dative of manifestation. The subject of appearances, named by the noun in the simple sentence, is a subject for someone who registers what it is going through. This requirement confines the range of nouns. It still permits them to transcend a situation, because just as things named by nouns can enter into other situations besides those named by a particular verb, I too can speak from within contexts different from those which provide the setting for any particular sentence, even though my way of transcending a context as a speaker, and remaining the same speaker in a new situation, is different from the way an object named by the noun goes beyond any one setting and appears again in another. The need for a speaker as a part of the context for naming sets limits therefore to the possibility of, say, sulfur to manifest itself. Sulfur has entered into registrations on earth, but whether it can be registered in its various ways in the Andromeda nebula is questionable. We can certainly report on it there by reading instruments, but report is not registration. If we or some other beings who can name things cannot get close enough to the Andromeda nebula, sulfur cannot be registered there.

The extreme in detachment from a context occurs when we allow a variable to replace nouns in sentences. Variables are supposed to refer to anything in any place, any time, and any context. To determine the values of a variable, we are supposed to scan everything and discover whether there are any objects that possess the predicates the sentence in question asserts of the variable. We as scanners are transformed into beings that survey everything from no particular point of view, and the variable, as a replacement for names, ranges over everything; the variable is a sign which, positively or negatively, refers to every being there is. If the speaker and the sign are taken this way, the concept of context becomes irrelevant, applicable only to those speakers who cannot reach this extreme of detachment and to languages that fall away from this purity. And from this absolute point of view we could claim, certainly, that we see things as they truly are, not as they appear to one limited perspective among many.

But from this absolute viewpoint we could only report about things, we could never register anything. We would behave as minds detached from sensibility and incapable of involving our thinking with what we perceive. Is this detached condition something real, or is it a construct fabricated by pushing a tendency of the mind—the pull away from a particular context—into an extremity which it can never realize? Nouns reflect the ability we have to go beyond a particular setting, but have we "nouned" ourselves to death? Nouns only work as implicated with verbs, thinking only works with perception, and transcending a context means being invariant in many contexts, not escaping all contexts whatsoever;

reporting is not detachable from registration. To isolate nouns, thought, and reporting is to make an abstract part into a concrete whole.

The complement to the noun is the verb, which pulls us into a context. The verb's particularity is shown in the time which is part of its signification, but it is also reflected in the complexity of the verb's structure, which attempts to assemble within itself many of the details of the event of manifestation. The verb picks up moods, adverbs, and auxiliaries. It also assembles prepositions, which in European languages are floating adverbs that become fixed as prepositions and allow the verb to govern more cases and express more of the momentary relations in the event which it names.[2] Indeed, the verb can serve as a miniature of the whole sentence if it acquires personal inflections in its structure, as in the Latin *scribet.* Here no independent noun is needed to register what we wish to say, the verb alone recapitulates the event. Of course the verb's attempt to capture all the details is never successful, and the identity of the speaker is again necessary to recover the concrete context of the sentence. The abstractive force of language remains; the verb never succeeds in totally expressing a situation, no more than the noun succeeds in completely escaping it.

The noun as subject also accepts modifiers, such as adjectives or relative clauses: "The tall man who crossed the street was hit by a car." But these modifiers are the residue of earlier verbal articulations, earlier apparitions, which are now packed into the noun as we move on to the event we wish to register with our present verb. The noun itself, if it has not been transformed into a pure variable, will imply certain attributes normally understood to be part of what it names: "dog" involves being a certain kind of animal which behaves in certain ways and has certain characteristics which it would be redundant to mention when making a statement about a dog. Such implications, parts of the meaning of the noun, are also the sediment of earlier verbal manifestations, but they do not explicitly come to life in the present sentence. In the present speech act, the noun names the object that could be found in some other context, while the verb names the way the object appears in this context and not another.

The verb, with its phenomenality, tends toward the registrational use of language, while the noun, with its emphasis on repeatability in new contexts, tends toward reporting. The verb moves toward evocation and the articulation of what we perceive, the noun tends toward reference.

The distinction between nouns and verbs, with the corresponding differentiation between a concrete situation and elements in it that can be found elsewhere, is a late development in language. In a more primitive state words are not distinguished into nouns and verbs, but occur as what we might call gerunds, verbal nouns. Such words name actions and cling to the situation that provides their utterance; they may even name things as activities. Curiously, the primitive stems of verbs, with their gerundial sense, survive in developed languages in the imperative mood, where the simple naming of the action or condition, without mention of a subject and with no grammatical articulation, is a kind of discrete suggestion that the addressee bring it about within the context in which it is expressed.[3]

Speech made up of gerunds does not have the crisp beginning and end to sentences that the contrast between nouns and verbs provides; the analogue to a sentence is an unravelling of various parts of the situation as its different aspects catch the attention of the speaker. And ontogeny recapitulates phylogeny, so both in baby talk and in evocation or articulating a perception we find ourselves naming successive events as they unfold continuously from one another, rather than asserting the distinct subject and predicate. This parataxis in speech follows closely the perceived event as it impresses itself on the speaker's mind; the lack of a noun, and the lack of a clear beginning and end of a statement, reflect a certain intellectual passiveness and receptivity in the speaker, who lets himself be led by what appears about him. This intellectual passivity does not imply that the speaker does not do anything about his situation. He may be engaged in changing it radically— building something, eating, going somewhere—but his thinking does not have the decisiveness and detachment that comes with the grammatical differentiations we are describing.

The ability to report, to refer to an action or condition in a context different from the one that encloses the speaker, is developed along with the ability to use words as names of things that can exist in other contexts besides our own; it arises with the ability to use nouns. To do this we must be able to create a context and not just accept one. The other context is created with our words, which now do more than articulate events in the setting which we, as spatial, temporal, and bodily beings, cannot at any moment really escape; we now have to establish a setting of which we are not a part but in which our words are supposed to find their referents. This, the power to report, calls for greater intellectual initiative.[4] And once the dimension of reporting has become opened to us, we begin also to register in a new way: we now know that a context can be transcended, and that what we register here and now can, later and elsewhere, be reported, so we register in a repeatable way, with precision and discreteness. We begin to employ nouns in an articulation of what is immediate to us because we anticipate reporting it later, using the same nouns again, when it is no longer immediate. We come to realize that there can be different contexts, and that our present situation, privileged and inescapable as it now is, will later become one context among many. If a language does not discriminate between nouns and verbs, if it employs the gerundial form in its speech, it tends to name only events implicated directly in the context of utterance.

Another grammatical form in which the verbal manifestation predominates and the noun or subject recedes is found in certain impersonal constructions, such as "it is raining," "it is getting dark (or warm, or cold)," *es schneit,* and the Latin *tonat, pluit, vesperascit.* This form is often used in European languages for describing the weather and other pervasive natural phenomena that seem to qualify completely the context of speech. They are not attributes or processes belonging to any particular thing; the speaker and everything about him get chilly when "it gets chilly." The unspecified "it" also functions in mentioning time: "it is Sunday," "it is three o'clock." Nothing particular is three o'clock, everything is. Secondly, the same construction is used in many languages to name the emergence of moods or emotions which, in contrast to the weather, well up from within the speaker, affect him primarily, and saturate the context from that source: *taedet me, piget me, dolet mihi, es freut mich.* The person involved in the feeling is put into an accusative or dative case. In English we use personal subjects for such verbs, as though the emotions were actions or characteristics we brought about through our own doing. Thirdly, the impersonal is sometimes used in verbs that announce the surfacing of ideas or opinions in one's mind, for example "it seems to me," *videtur mihi,* and the interesting case of "methinks," in which "me" is in the dative. This verb, which also survives in the German impersonal *es dünkt mich,* is not the same as our present verb "to think," although it became confused with it in Middle English. Its meaning is like that of "seems," and the impersonal construction of both implies that we do not generate the thoughts and appearances we have, but that they come to us. (Of course once thoughts are there we can do things with them: arrange, collect, focus, revive them and the like, and this activity of which we are indeed the agents is expressed in the verb which is now used in English for thinking, and which has the same stem as the German *denken.* But this activity, which corresponds to what we have called the syntactical dimension of speech, must be preceded by the passivity of seeming, "methinks," and *dünken,* which corresponds to what we have called the lexical aspect.) A fourth category of impersonals, one similar to that of verbs naming the emergence of appearances and thoughts in an individual, is made up of verbs that name the presence of opinions among people generally. *Dicitur, traditur, creditur, dokei, phainetai,* "it is said," *on dit, man sagt,* are examples of this. No particular person is identified as the one responsible for the opinion; it merely floats into view, almost like the weather which materializes without an agent. Finally a fifth class of impersonals is made up of verbs like *decet, licet, opus est,* the Greek *dei,* and the French *il faut,* words that express necessity (moral and natural), need, permission, and the like. They express how things have to be, how they ought to be, or how they are permitted to be, and no one in the context of discourse is the subject-agent for them.

There is a temptation, to which E. C. Woodcock has succumbed, to think that impersonal verbs must have an implied subject. After observing that impersonals have only a third person singular ending, he says: "This does not mean that they have no 'subject', for the activity denoted by the third-personal verbal inflection must be performed by someone or something, even if the speaker does not know what it is." He then continues: "The subject may be assumed to be the noun implied in the root of the verb. With those impersonal verbs of active form which denote the activities of phenomena, such as *tonat,* 'it thunders'; *pluit,* 'it rains'; *ningit,* 'it snows'; *vesperascit,* 'the shades of evening fall'; etc., the subjects are 'thunder', 'rain', 'snow', 'evening', etc."[5] Woodcock reads the noun and verb structure into this more elementary form of language.

However, his suggestion is interesting and by developing it we may be able to show the peculiarities of words, impersonals and gerundials alike, that name events. Suppose we try to make the subject of the impersonals explicit and say "the thunder thunders," "the rain rains," "my grief grieves me," and "shame shames." We tug at the verb and pull out a noun, and make it look like one of our standard sentences. But what have we obtained as an agent in our subject? What is thunder but the thundering? What is rain but the raining, and grief but the grieving? We have pulled out a dummy subject. It is not like the subject in "The man walked across the street," because the man can be and do other things besides walk across the street, and he can still be a man if he does not cross the street at all. But rain cannot fail to rain down if it is to be itself, and it really cannot do anything else except rain. But can't rain also make the grass grow, and can't grief, besides grieving, also make me miss an appointment? Not really, because it is only as raining down that rain makes the grass grow; it does not do it as an agent distinct from raining down—whereas a man who crosses the street can also read a newspaper, and his reading is an action quite distinct from crossing the road. His being is not exhausted in crossing the street, but the being of rain is exhausted in raining. Any further consequences it brings about are achieved by its raining, not by itself as a subject distinguishable from the raining. Therefore it would, strictly speaking, be meaningless to say "The rain is not raining" or "The wind is not blowing"—although we can say "The man is not reading"—because there is no rain if it is not raining and no wind if it is not blowing. Rain and raining are the same.

No independent noun is needed for such impersonal verbs because the verb names the anonymous emergence of a process. There is no subject which appears in the manifestation that the verb names; the event simply appears, and any putative subject (my grief, *taedet me*) is merely one of the appendages of it. The impersonal verb is not really different from a gerund used to name an action going on before us. The unspecified "it" and other forms of the third person singular are added to make the naming of the event conform to normal sentence structure, since the more elementary form of speech now has to find its place among sentences that have nouns and verbs.

Moreover, this is not just a peculiar fact about languages. It reflects the way things appear. There are some beings, and there are certain levels in the presentation of all beings, which are appropriately named as anonymous manifestations. They are states or processes which do not have clear differentiations. Our experience of them is associative and continuous, and they are associative and continuous. It is impossible for us to say how many parts there are in the rain that is raining and in the grief that floods in upon us; it is not even easy to say whether a new rain, after a period of sunshine, or another round of sorrow after an interlude in which it is forgotten, is numerically different from the earlier one or just an interrupted continuation of it. Likewise, is the present *non decet* a different one from that which existed last year? There can even be a flooding of red, or a flooding of friendship, or a flooding of Charles de Gaulle. We do go beyond such experience and being when we make discrete identifications in perception and speech, but the anonymous, continuous presences persist as a foundation for what is built upon them. In our languages we are urged by grammar to go beyond the continuous manifestation to its discrete ingredients, while less developed languages may incline their speakers to stay with the verbal process, but both elements are at work in what can be experienced.

The occurrences which seem to come about without an agent are sometimes, in poetry and in pagan religion, attributed to a deity or a preternatural being. Jupiter may be said to be thundering, and Neptune causes storms; when a war breaks out, Mars may be said to move into action; the Muses, daughters of Memory, may be the ones who bring things to mind; and circumstances may be as they are because of agreements made by certain gods. The anonymous emergence of the processes named by impersonals is mysterious, something like fortune or luck in life, and men have worshipped the beings that were said to be behind such events. Part of the sense of Christianity is to assert that there is nothing in such things to be worshipped, that what St. Paul calls the "elements of the world" and the "principalities and powers" do not deserve adoration, that men are no longer religiously subordinated to them because of what has been achieved by Christ (Colossians 2:8-15). Thus the continuous occurrences associated with gerundials and impersonals are not only the foundations for more distinct experience and thought; some of them are also involved in what is enigmatic in our experience, and some are related to the religious and its theological articulation.

The adhesion of gerundials to the context in which they are spoken is not caused just by the overriding interest the speakers have in their immediate environment; it is also caused by the continuous character of the processes such words designate. Even though it may not be raining now, the rain we had earlier may be considered as simply coming back, after an interruption, when it begins to rain again. The raining is continuous with our present context, not discretely separated from it as, say, an identifiable individual substance might be. A language immersed in gerundials tends not to report or create new contexts; it names even elapsed events as paratactic with what is going on now.

The isolating force of nouns as subjects of sentences breaks this continuity of being and manifestation and, at the same time, breaks the simple continuity of speech into sentences with definite beginnings and ends. This move allows us to create a context of reference discontinuous with our own and permits us to report. We can do this not only because of linguistic evolution, but also because being can be discrete as well as continuous, and lends itself, in each of these states, to a corresponding kind of naming.

Finally, it will become necessary for us to discuss the gerund *par excellence*, "being." What is its putative subject, the subject of Parmenides' impersonal *esti*? What event does "being" name, and how is it related to the events of "raining," "grieving," *licet, decet,* the Greek *dei,* and the like? How can being straddle continuity and discreteness, cover the present context as well as any distant one we report about, and include not only anything that can be named, but the act of naming and the name itself?

Notes

1. William J. Entwistle, *Aspects of Language* (London: Faber and Faber, 1953), p. 168; see also pp. 145, 155, 187. I am grateful to George Siefert for bringing Entwistle's book, and some linguistic materials related to it, to my attention.

2. See Entwistle, *Aspects of Language,* p. 223, and E. C. Woodcock, *A New Latin Syntax* (Cambridge: Harvard University Press, 1959), p. 3. In Chinese, prepositions are derived not from "adverbs" but directly from verbs; they emerge not from words that modify a verb, but from other verbs that are added to the main verb.

3. See Entwistle, *Aspects of Language,* pp. 212, 218-19. On gerundials see pp. 168, 228, 230. Also Ernest Fenollosa, *The Chinese Written Character as a Medium for Poetry,* ed. E. Pound (San Francisco: City Lights Books, 1936), p. 28: "We should be ware of English grammar, its hard parts of speech, and its lazy satisfaction with nouns and adjectives. We should seek and at least bear in mind the verbal undertone of each noun."

4. See Samuel Johnson, *A Journey to the Western Islands of Scotland,* ed. R. W. Chapman (New York: Oxford University Press, 1970), p. 134: "Whatever withdraws us from the power of our senses; whatever makes the past, the distant, or the future predominate over the present, advances us in the dignity of human beings."

5. Woodcock, *A New Latin Syntax,* p. 166.

CHAPTER 3

How Names Are Given

Names have been classified into such categories as common and proper, relative (father-son) and nonrelative, positive and negative, connotative and denotative, concrete and abstract. They have been defined as signs which identify objects, signs which indicate objects, signs which distinguish an object from other things, words used to establish a reference, and as concealed descriptions of what they name. The classification of names does not explain what they are, of course, but the definitions have not done so either.

These definitions fail in two ways. Names are sometimes defined in terms of, and in contrast to, other parts of the sentence, like grammatical particles and words which are supposed to express concepts. Such a procedure may illuminate how names function, but it cannot define them, because sentences, grammar, and concept-expressions presuppose names. Naming sets the horizon for such things, and it would be redundant to define names in terms of them. It would be an exercise in the classification of terms, not a definition of names. On the other hand, to say names identify or indicate an object does not show how they differ from a signal or a mark that announces the presence of an object or makes us think of it, and distinguishes that object from others. A characteristic noise or odor associated with the object would do as much. In the first case, there is an attempt to define names while taking naming for granted, in the second an attempt to define names while not acknowledging naming. The first never gets outside the context of names—which is also the context of language and sentences—and the second never reaches it. The way these two explanations fail shows, however, that the issue of naming marks the transition from nonlinguistic to linguistic and sentential signs.

Our procedure will be to show how the "matter" of a sign associated with an object becomes a name when it receives the "form" of the play of presence and absence. This transition is analogous to a sound's becoming a phoneme when it receives the "form" of binary opposition which locates it within a language structure, a theme we shall examine in chapter seven.

Association is usually treated in terms of what is presented to us: one object, through similarity, contiguity, or succession, is said to bring another object to mind. But such a treatment makes the percipient too much a rigid spectator. In association, the self is associative too; the associative pull may not only draw other things to mind, but may prompt me to do certain things. Someone drawing out a cigarette may prompt me to take out my lighter. The appearance of an irritating person may make me angry, the presence of a certain animal may make me fearful, even though neither of these may yet have done anything, this time at least, to cause my anger or fear. I may respond to something by a certain stylized motion of my arms, face, head, or other members. And finally I may respond by making a certain kind of sound. Making such a sound would be no different from any other reaction to the object. Someone else might infer from the sound that the object is present, just as one might infer from a certain kind of bark that the dog's master has appeared, but in neither case is this someone else referred to the object, even though his attention is drawn to it. Neither case involves sounds as names.

Association always involves a move into some sort of absence; we fish the associated out of what is *not* available for perception. We are prompted by what is present to bring to mind something absent. The associating object is present, the associated is absent; if the latter were not absent, we would speak of a continued perception, not an association. Now if the associated part of the pair is a behavior we react with or a sound we are to make, this response too is at first absent when the associating part appears to us; the response is something we are drawn to do. The associative pull brings our response into being.

But association does not occur in the cool detachment we have suggested by our description so far; it is always immersed in desire or rejection, pleasure or pain. Things suggest other things because we desire them and wish to have them present, or because we fear them and want to be warned of their imminence; even the original similarities, contiguities, and successions were noticed, and hence served as a base for associations, because they were of some affective interest to us. Suppose, then, that I experience a need for something: a desire for food, water, for someone or some place. In this condition I may utter the sound associated with the object; the sound is solicited not simply by the object, but by my felt desire for it. The sound is part of an attempt to make the object present, at least in fantasy. I bring about the items associated with the object which are in my power to bring about—and the sound is always mine to make—in the hope that the object will come too. The sound is both a call to the object and a symptom of my desire. The sound can still occur when the object becomes present and my desire is gratified; it then accompanies the object and is a symptom of my gratification. It remains supported by these two coordinated elements, the object and my desire. Both elements are mentioned by Aristotle as essential to what he calls "voice," the production of sound by a living thing: voice is an indication of pleasure and pain (*Politics* I. 2. 1253a11); and it can be produced only by creatures "using fantasy," because voice "indicates" something (*De Anima* II. 8. 420b32-33).

In the early years of life, the infant lives in such association and its voice summons its mother, food, and other things it desires. From the beginning, however, the absence that characterizes association is at work, because there is always some delay and frustration before the infant's desire is gratified; the rhythmic, consistent experience of such delay and gratification is as important for the healthy development of the infant as is the actual satisfaction of its needs. The child begins to differentiate between himself and other things as he begins to realize that although the voice is always his to use, the gratification is not his to give. The initial self and objects are, of course, pervaded with pleasure and pain; there is no object but what gratifies or discomforts, no self except what enjoys or suffers. Desire and delayed gratification gradually establish the difference between self and other, but the role of the voice and other signals is also necessary, and may be considered as the initial emergence of what psychoanalytic theory calls ego functions, as opposed to instinctual drives. Clustered around the voice are the desires which it signals, the gratifying object which it summons, the dative to whom the summons is directed, the space it covers, and the stretch of time over which it is effective. These differentiations take place for the initiator of the voice as he gradually becomes its controller and begins to master the absences over which it ranges.

So far in the life of the child there is no true experience of presence and absence; there is only experience of gratification and deprivation. Unless a gratifying object is forgotten and the desire for it extinguished, or unless another gratification takes over, the loss of what gives pleasure is felt as deprivation and causes anger or grief, of which the voice can be a symptom. Separation is not tolerated; if what is lost is to be thought of at all, it is as something to be pulled back toward gratification. The only alternative is oblivion. And besides pain at the loss of pleasure, there is fear about its return. Inability to accept separation is also uncertainty about regaining the gratification after it disappears. The importance of consistent delay and gratification for a child lies in getting him used to mastering succession, to tolerating separation without panic, and in engendering confidence that what he desires will come back.[1]

For painful objects, confrontation and release are the correlates to gratification and deprivation, but here it is the presence and not the loss that has to be mastered. The sufferer must come to realize that he is not identified with his affliction and that he will be released from it. The sense of succession is a part of this, as it is a part of accepting separation: time will distinguish him from his present condition, and so what distresses him now becomes appreciated as *only* present. But until this dissociation is achieved, confrontation with the painful cannot be tolerated, and our only concern is to bring about release, just as our only way of handling deprivation is by the return of what gratifies.

Maturation involves becoming capable of tolerating the loss of what is pleasurable. As time goes on, and if things go well, we develop a basic trust that what has left us will return again. Although a step toward naming, this is not naming itself. At this point we do not think of the desirable object as somewhere else when it is lost; it has simply evaporated and it will materialize again, in a kind of interrupted continuity. Even if we have come to fabricate a certain stylized sound with the gratification and loss, we do not yet name what we have.

Nor is the further step of realizing that an object continues to exist when it leaves us equivalent to naming the object. As mobility is developed, together with a sense of space and a sense of the permanence of things, we may set out in search of what we desire and expect to find it at some place or other; if we make our accustomed sound when looking for and finding the item, we may be on the verge of naming, but still not into it.

A desirable or distressing thing becomes a nameable thing when its affective spell is broken and we become indifferent to its gratification or loss, confrontation or release. True, the naming may in fact involve excitement, but it does not as such require it. We may passionately talk about something; but we may also dispassionately discuss it, and our naming is nonetheless naming when we do so. Naming opens a dimension where, in principle, our positive and negative affectivity about something can converge toward zero, even when we have the object in mind. Our naming may become the servant of our passions; it may be used as a device to arrange more intricate and farther delayed gratification, or it may be a means of complicated defense against confrontations. But although naming may be so exploited almost all the time, naming as such does not need to be utilitarian; it can be done for its own sake. It can be indifferent even to remote gratification and loss, confrontation and release.

Indifference to presence and absence is a characteristic of naming; can we explain why? Can we explain what naming is, that it should be so characterized? When we name something which is before us, we are also aware of the possibility of its not being before us, of its being somewhere else. Since this possibility is given to us, its foil is also given: we are likewise aware of the presence of the object, that it *is* here and not elsewhere. We do not just enjoy the object; "between" the object and us, "in addition to" the object, there is this dimension of the thing's ability to be somewhere else now, and also the actuality of its being here. This is the extra element that establishes names. This dimension reveals the object as

indifferent to being present or absent; it would be the same thing
whether it is presented or not. The indifference of the object to
presence and absence is then reflected in an indifference on our
part to its availability or loss, for we recognize that the object does
remain itself whether we enjoy it or not. We now can appreciate the
object "objectively," apart from what it does for or against us. And
the sound we have been making in association with the object can
now become its name.

We might also say that a directly named object is an object appreciated *as present*. The "as present" does not, of course, signify a
particular feature of the object, like its being red or solid or sticky; it
determines the object as a whole, as being here before me while I
am able to name it. Furthermore, this "as present" is appreciated
precisely as "not being absent" now, while I have the thing before
me. The dimension of possible but excluded absence is part of the
sense of presence; it is the couple "presence-absence" that comes
between me and the object and makes the object nameable. Therefore, instead of discussing "the object as present," as we have been
doing, we might better say "the object as presentable" when we
identify what makes the object subject to names. This term, the "as
presentable," includes both presence and absence and the play
between them.[2]

So far we have been describing how we name an object which is
actually present to us. How does naming work when the object is
absent? If the play of presence and absence has not yet intruded
between the object and us, we find it hard to bring the object to
mind without reacting with either positive or negative affectivity
toward it. We become excited when we think of it, and any sounds
we utter are part of a response to loss, release, or anxiety. But the
indifference to presence and absence allows us to speak of the
object as remaining itself and keeping all its characteristics when it
is not available to us. Furthermore, the pleasure of discoursing
about an object is as complete when carried on in absence as in
presence. It is in fact easier to talk about something, to describe it
more thoroughly and to draw out its implications, when the object
is not present. For Plato, to have the *eidos*, the "look" of an object in
speech, is far better than to have the object in perception.

When we name something absent, we do name what is absent.

We do not name a copy, an image, a phantasm, or some other present representative of it.[3] Names stretch into what is not here. They can do so because they are constituted precisely as the masters of both the presence and the absence of what they name. Even when they name what is present, they do so with a sense of its capacity to be not present, and it is the thing as exercising this other capacity, the thing as absent, which they name in reports about objects that are not before us. It is the object which is absent but still appreciated "as presentable" that we name; when naming the absent, we refer to it as it would be presented to anyone, to any dative, were the loss of the object to be overcome.

When we do have an object present, we have it given in only some of its ways of being presentable. When we speak of it in its absence, we can collect into our discourse all its ways of being given, and our speech may be more adequate to the object than is our experience of it, even though what we say must always be brought back to experience for verification. In our attempt to say everything necessary about the object, we might try to express its exhaustive presentability, to say how it would be presented to an ideal observer who is not limited by a context of manifestation, as we always are. We might aim at this ideal of thorough knowledge, which is made possible as an ideal only by our ability to talk about things in their absence. But if we claim that this ideal is to be the norm for what things are, and allow it to substitute for thoughtful perception in deciding what is true, we would be enlisting with Plato and forgetting that what we can say about things begins and ends in our experience of them. Such a conception of naming would involve not an indifference to presence and absence but a preference for the absent; it helps account for Plato's description of philosophy as the practice of dying, the preparation for a viewpoint which can quite definitely only be achieved "somewhere else" (*Phaedo* 67E; see 64, 66-67, 80E). To implicate names irrevocably with presence, however, is to take them as bringing to completion the desirability of things and the gratification we have in them. Names bring about a new excellence in things, their truthfulness. This perfection does not compete with any other desirability a thing has, nor is it added to it independently, as something extra; rather, it makes the goodness of the thing become a known and named goodness, when the thing is named.[4] Part of the way names accomplish this is by allowing us to possess, in speech, things which are absent; but the names always belong back with the things they bring to completion.

Naming gives us a kind of mastery and objectivity over the affective charge things have, but it does not eliminate it. It enhances the desirableness of things by articulating them and making them gratifying in differentiated and subtle ways; it can also articulate what is painful and make possible deeper suffering and anxiety. Naming rests precariously atop the strong forces of gratification and loss, confrontation and release, and frequently enough it is overcome by them. The substrate for naming floods through, and our words, tumbling around, cease to be names any longer. They cease telling anyone else about the things at issue and become once again signals of our feelings and of the objects causing them. We are back in associated sounds. Grammar and consistency also suffer in these circumstances. When talking to someone, it is important to sense whether his words are names or symptoms, but it is sometimes difficult to do so because he will almost never be able to tell you which they are.

The occurrence of the "as presentable" between the object and its dative, the one who becomes able to name the object, is also a condition for the thing's entering into articulated facts or states of affairs and subsequently into propositions. When the object is named, it becomes ready for grammar. Grammatical and syntactical operations, like combination, predication, disjunction, or collection, can be carried out only upon things that have become named; and the naming transformation itself cannot be conceived as a grammatical or syntactical operation. What we do with things after we have named them is to execute the linkage which we have described, in our first chapter, as the syntactical element in speech.

Such articulation does not, of course, do anything to the object in the sense that squeezing, painting, or cutting it does; it is an operation carried out in another dimension. Even when we deal with the object in a prephilosophical way, we are familiar with this dimension of presencing and absencing; we often refer to it, and we recognize the difference between an object's being around and its not being there. But this familiarity is only casual and provisional, and we do not make this dimension our explicit theme. We do not truly name presence and absence as such, because our real interest is with the object named, not with the dimensions and differences that allow it to be named. Part of doing philosophy is to change this direction of interest, to turn from the thing named and from its features to the structures in the dimension of presence and absence that make naming and articulating possible: to show how there can be an object and how it can have features, and to clarify what sort of operations registration and reporting are. Our prephilosophical acquaintance with this domain is so casual that we think there are only one or two gross distinctions that can be made in it, and that they are of little substance. But the structural possibilities in presence, absence, and identity are delicate and complex, and many necessities can be registered in them which illuminate what we take for granted in our experience of things.

Finally, the naming aspect of words is not found only in nouns or in the subjects of sentences. Adjectives, verbs, adverbs, predicates, all have a naming component. So far in our analysis we have not distinguished between nouns and adjectives, for example, or subjects and predicates, because we have not yet begun to talk about grammar sufficiently. But naming as we have described it applies to words like "John," "red," "horse," "stutters," and "mournfully"; it applies to the lexical core which all such words have and which cuts across their grammatical differences. I can acquire the naming distance to someone's behavior of stuttering as much as to red or to houses or to my uncle; the fact that any word, even a verb or an adverb, can be made into a noun is a grammatical indication of this. The only words that do not have a naming element like that of "John" or "stutters" are sheer grammatical particles, like some prepositions or the copula "is." The function of such words seems to be exhausted in linkage. However, although they do not name immediately, as the names of things and features do, they still have a naming function of a special and mediated sort, a kind of second-level naming, which works in the verification of propositions, as we shall see in chapter ten.

Notes

1. On separation, anxiety, ambiguity, the identity of objects and the identity of the self as structural elements in human development, see Elizabeth R. Zetzel and W. W. Meissner, *Basic Concepts of Psychoanalytic Psychiatry* (New York: Basic Books, 1973), esp. chapters 11-13.

2. My analysis of naming is developed on the basis of Husserl's concept of the blend of empty and filled intentions, which he uses to explain our ability to recognize the identity of things. See *Logical Investigations*, trans. J. N. Findlay (New York: Humanities Press, 1970), Investigation I, §9-§16; Investigation VI, §5-§10, §40.

3. On words as used to intend what is not present, see Martin Heidegger, *Logik: Die Frage nach der Wahrheit*, Collected Works, vol. 21 (Frankfurt: Klostermann, 1976), pp. 101-114.

4. Gertrude Stein, *Lectures in America* (New York: Vintage Books, 1975), p. 231: "A name of anything is not interesting because once you know its name the enjoyment of naming it is over. . . ." p. 236-37: "Now that was a thing that I too felt in me. The need of making it be a thing that could be named without using its name. After all one had known its name anything's name for so long, and so the name was not new but the thing being alive was always new."

CHAPTER 4

A Sequence of Indications

The various stages involved in naming are reflected in the sequence of what we might call indicative terms. At the first and most elementary level we have *cries,* sounds which signal that something alarming or exciting is affecting the one who makes them. They signal a disturbance, whether pleasant or painful. Secondly, *exclamations* can be considered as sounds made to alert someone else about something noteworthy appearing in the space common to the exclaimer and the one addressed. They tell us to pay attention; they signal something prominent without saying what it is, but the sudden change in the context makes it clear what we are being alerted to. Utterances like "look," "watch out," "heads up," "hey," or just a shout will do this, and the context provides what they signal: a car headed toward us, a yellowjacket, a puddle, a lion charging out of the woods. Exclamations are also usually spontaneous cries that signal a disturbance for the one making them, and hence they can overlap with our first category, but in addition they alert someone el.e to something intruding on all concerned. Thirdly, *demonstratives* also draw someone's attention to something, but they always, explicitly or implicitly, connote the kind of thing we are pointing to. We usually say "this house," "this red color," "this shape," or "this illness"; but if we were to say merely "this," it is always clear, or can be made clear, from other things we have said or from the general interest the interlocutors have at the moment, what kind of thing "this" indicates. As speakers we are more active when we use demonstratives; we specify what kind of thing we pick out. In exclamations we just alert the others and let the context specify what is important. We do not specify a kind. There is practically no "hermeneutic horizon" for exclamations, but there is a very confining one for demonstratives. Also, in demonstratives any vestige of a cry of alarm—our first category, which can also occur in exclamations—is washed away. The use of demonstratives is entirely in the context of naming; more precisely, it refers to something present to us, and is used in registrations.

Fourth and last, *the definite article* also picks out a particular object, but one which is absent; it works in reporting. Here the kind of thing we are referring to is of paramount importance and has to be made explicit. It is more dominant here than in the use of demonstratives, where it could be left implicit. "The man who bought my car," "the storm we had yesterday," "the flower pot"; we not only specify the kind of thing, but often add a characteristic that identifies it in its individuality. This added character may be left undetermined if what we have been saying, or our general interest at the moment, specifies it: "the car" mentioned in a family context will mean the family car.[1] However, the kind of thing "the" prefaces can never be left unstated, as it can in the use of "this." We must add these factors, the kind and the identifying characteristic, to the definite article because the object is not there before us to identify itself. We have to create the entire context with our words. And the "cry of alarm" is even farther removed from the definite article than it is from demonstratives. Of course, we can refer to "the man who bought my car" only because we might have, in principle, at one time been able to say "This man is buying my car." As reports involve the possibility of registration, and naming the absent involves the possibility of naming the same thing while it is present, so the definite article involves the possibility of using demonstratives to refer to the same object.

Not only the four levels, but the transitions from one to the next are worthy of study. Demonstratives give way to the definite article when we move from naming what is present to naming what is absent. Exclamations give way to demonstratives when we move from an attitude of reacting to things to one of speaking about them. An exclamation does not prepare what it signals to be a part of a sentence or proposition; it does not make the object ready for grammar; we do not go on to talk about it, and the exclamation itself is not a grammatical part of a sentence. But a demonstrative does establish a reference and it is a part of a sentence. Finally, cries of alarm give way to exclamations when we transcend our own sensibility, when we appreciate the intrusion as one which is there for others as well as for ourselves.

Clearly, demonstratives involve a fully developed system of names. They implicitly or explicitly involve a discrimination of kinds, which can be achieved only with names, and the speaker using demonstratives comes equipped with a store of categories that he brings to his perception: he is active, even aggressive; he means *this*. Equally clearly, the cry of alarm, on our first level, does not involve names. It is entirely a signal of pleasure or pain in the one making it. But what about exclamations? They are more than private signals; they recognize a common space, the presence of others, and an interest others will have in what is intruding. Through them we draw the attention of others to the prominent object, not to ourselves as suffering or enjoying something. And yet exclamations do stand outside sentences and involve no grammar. How are we to describe them? Exclamations express something which remains in demonstratives: they express an undetermined interest in what is intruding, a receptivity to what is prominent in the space around us. This is an attitude of acceptance which continues to subsist when we move to demonstratives but do not become too hasty in imposing our names of kinds, our specifications, on what is before us. Sometimes we may want insistently to say our piece and take our position; the quick imposition of a category can be a mark of decisiveness. But it can also be a mark of insensitivity and lack of curiosity. There should be a residue of the exclamatory when we begin to register things and facts. It reflects an elemental interest and acceptance of things that remains alive when we begin to talk about them. It provides the flexibility in which a sense of metaphor and a feeling for the nuance survive. This residue cannot appear in any of the words or grammatical parts of the sentence itself, but perhaps it can appear in the exclamation sign, which is the appropriate punctuation mark for registrations, whereas the period, calm and completed, is more apt for punctuating reports.[2]

In terms of the distinctions made so far, there are two ways in which words can distort what we wish to name. At one extreme, names may regress to being symptoms of our affectivity if the naming function becomes overcome by the pleasure or pain aroused by what we are concerned with. Actually, names always have an element of affectivity and serve as symptoms, even when they are working quite well to identify objects. The way our attention moves, the kinds of association that arise in our speech as we continue to talk about something betray what is interesting to us and reveal how we are made up emotionally; someone trying to figure us out may be interested more in our speech as a symptom than in what it tells him about the world: "I don't understand everything you say," asserts the unlettered Milly Henning to Hyacinth Robinson, "but I understand everything you hide" (Henry James, *The Princess Casamassima*, chapter 41). This symptomatic aspect of speech need not harm the objectivity of what we say; it accompanies every discourse, since every speech is made by someone who has a particular character, history, and fund of associations. But sometimes it does overcome a speech, and what is said can then be practically worthless as a report or registration of how things are.

Secondly, at the other extreme, our words may fail to rest on any affective response to things. We simply make use of terms we pick up from others. Our speech is rigid and does not grow out of a sensitive involvement in what we refer to. We have never ourselves reacted to the good or the repulsive in what we discuss, so our words remain external to it. The object has never exercised any associative pulls for us, we have never discovered any similarities and identities it enters into. We could not disclose anything essential about the object; if we merely repeat what others say, we do not become able to discriminate between the essentials and the coincidentals of the object, and we have no authority in regard to it. It is not worthwhile for anyone to cite our opinion. Everything has its pleasure and pain: colors, places, scientific experiments, the moon, government, mathematical proofs, light and darkness, water. Unless we have responded to such things, unless we have made use of the exclamatory in regard to them, we cannot contribute to what is to be said about them.

Both these ways of slanting the use of names are very common in speech. There are some users of language who seldom say anything that is not more a symptom of feeling and attitudes than a report of fact, and the repetition of what others assert about things makes up a large part of what most of us have to say. Furthermore, there is no criterion, no way of telling the difference between defective and authentic naming, except to be acquainted with the issue ourselves and to see that what is being said does not do it justice, and to have had enough experience with people to know the many ways in which speech can fall short of what it pretends to be. Nothing will do this for us if we cannot do it ourselves.

In chapter two we distinguished between speech based on gerundial forms and speech broken up into identifiable sentences with nouns and verbs. How do these distinctions fit with those made in our discussion of naming? Nouns obviously belong with demonstratives and definite articles; nouns name things that can be found to appear in other contexts than the immediate setting in which they are used. Verbs, since they name a manifestation, are more tied to a particular context and try to reconstitute it by accumulating many of its details. There is an element of the exclamatory in verbs when they are used to register; they have a sense of the imperative, "Look what's going on!" In registration they pull their noun-subjects into this action. However, they do enjoy a naming function and can report the manifestation even when it is no longer going on, or if it occurs somewhere else.

The kind of elementary speech in which gerunds predominate is less capable of being freed from exclamation. It adheres much more closely to the context of manifestation and of speech; it alerts to what is going on, and even when it tries to speak of something absent, its discourse seems to bring the manifestation back again. It carries a strong affective charge and is largely ruled by association. However, it is not just exclamation, because it has developed words that are distinguishable from one another; even though it may employ agglutination or agglomeration to a large extent, it does have some grammar; and it does associate certain words or word stems with certain kinds of appearances. Gerundial speech straddles exclamations and a rudimentary form of the demonstrative. It does not reach a distinct sense of demonstratives because it cannot identify a particular as an individual case of its kind; the sense of general category and individual instance is not yet available.

Speech used to accompany action is another interesting case. It is obviously implicated in the immediate situation, because that is where the performance takes place. It is made up largely of exclamations and imperatives, punctuated by expressions of pleasure or pain. The agents know more or less what they are to do, but exclamations alert them to items that have to be taken into account, while imperatives may adjust the movement of the action this way and that as circumstances require. The imperative mentions a part of the action that has to be brought into being, the exclamation indicates beings that must be absorbed into what is going on. At times the action may be held in abeyance while some discussion of the facts takes place, but this registration or report is strictly utilitarian, subordinated to getting the job done. Demonstratives might be used in such interruptions of the process, but they have little place—except as subordinated to imperatives—in the heat of action, where exclamations suffice. If someone were to use demonstratives in the course of the performance, he would imply that the addressee does not know how to carry out his part of the action and needs more than to be alerted to what is conspicuously relevant to his task; the work has to be suspended while he is given explicit instructions about what is going on.

The employment of language as a part of doing things is not a marginal or derivative way of using speech. As Heidegger has shown, language is first used in this utilitarian manner; even statements that seem to express the contemplation of facts are usually expressions of how our involvement with things proceeds: "The chalk is brittle" or "The roses are blooming" are remarks made first and foremost while we are writing on the blackboard or tending the garden, and they are part of these processes.[3] They require an adjustment in the way they are made if they are to become theoretical statements whose primary function is the disclosure of facts, the articulation of an object and its features. Such an adjustment is possible, of course, and often occurs; but the need for it has been overlooked, Heidegger claims, by philosophy, which has concentrated on the theoretical report as primary and has neglected the active use of language from which such reports arise; philosophy has consequently also neglected the elementary kind of disclosure which occurs in action and underlies the emergence of propositional truth.

The sequence of cries, exclamations, demonstratives, and the definite article has taken us through various levels of transcendence in the use of words. Each of these involves a special kind of absence. The sequence can be extended into still more intense forms of absence; we can move, for example, into the names of fictional entities and into the models and constructs used in science. The names of fictions, such as "Gulliver," refer to things in a context that we could not, in principle, actually enter. The nonfictional use of the definite article, which exploits the pull of nouns away from the present context in which we speak, permits us to identify objects that we may not for the moment directly experience but that are familiar to us: "My uncle is out selling the house." By enumerating enough features and by relating an object to things or persons we are acquainted with, we can identify objects we have never actually experienced but which have been reported to us: "Henry IV stood in the snow at Canossa." Fictional references go one step further: they identify someone or something in a context that no one has ever been in; moreover, the context is presented as not inhabitable by any of "us." It is "elsewhere" in a much more radical sense than something long ago and far away. Speaking about such contexts is structurally different from transmitting a report, but it is not hard to see that it exploits the kind of mastery over absence that reporting and reference give us. If names were not established by the play of presence and absence, fictional accounts would not be possible. This is not to say that fictions chronologically follow reports, that a child first controls the latter and then learns the former. The contrasts are structural, not genetic. At the beginning a child's sense of absence—as well as his sense of the corresponding presences—is undifferentiated, and the fictional is not clearly distinguished from the reported; but the distinction must be recognized as time goes on. Furthermore, there are differences even within the fictional: the structures of presence and absence at work in identifying figures we see in plays—Falstaff, for example—are different from the structures that operate in fictional things named only in narrative. The first have to be imitable in a way the second do not.

To name constructs in science is even more complicated in its manipulation of absence. Such scientific referents, though not perceivable themselves, are to be related to observable objects and events; they enter indirectly into our context of experience and speech. Furthermore, talk about them is embedded in theoretical axioms and laws, which at least in part are generalizations derived from experience. Constructs are usually acknowledged to be unlike those things with which we are familiar, and yet they have effects we can register. There is a curious mixture of the real and the constructed, an unusual combination of both presences and absences, in the establishment of such objects of reference. Once again, however, it is only because names range over the present and the absent that such scientific reference to constructs is possible.

Notes

1. See Peter Strawson, *Subject and Predicate in Logic and Grammar* (London: Methuen, 1974), p. 43; chapter 2 is entitled: "Proper Names—and Others."

2. On exclamation points, periods, and question marks, see Robert Sokolowski, *Husserlian Meditations: How Words Present Things* (Evanston: Northwestern University Press, 1974), pp. 234-35, 249.

3. *Logik: Die Frage nach der Wahrheit*, Collected Works, vol. 21 (Frankfurt: Klostermann, 1976), pp. 157-58.

CHAPTER 5

The Origins of Syntax

Once objects are named, it becomes possible to do certain things with them. The expression of such performances and of the structures they establish is found in the syntactical aspect of sentences. But before analyzing syntax and what it expresses, we must discuss the more elementary performances upon which it rests and of which it is the completion. This will be analogous to our discussion of gratification and loss as a preparation for naming.

We can take an object "as" something either by using it or by enjoying it in a certain way. I can take a stone as a doorstop when I use it to keep the door open; I could do the same with a shoe. I can take a leaf of mint as sweet when I smell it or chew it; I can take a patch of grass as soft when I lie down on it. The first performance is more active than the second because it involves my making use of an object, while the other simply lets the object affect me, but some activity is present in both. Even in the second I have to take steps to allow the object to carry out its work. I appreciate the difference between the object and the object as affecting me in a certain way.

No words are needed for either of these activities to come to pass. The objects do not have to be named. Still, the process of "taking as" installs a distinction between the object and the way it is taken, whether in use or in enjoyment. We do not start with an object and then add a use or affection to it; the distinction engenders both the object and its aspect conjointly. Nor must the agent who inserts the distinction have a word to express it; *we* can say he takes the shoe as a doorstop or the mint as sweet, but *he* simply takes them in such ways. He engenders the distinction and we find the word for it. We in turn, we who use the word "as," do not originate the distinction. We accept it from someone who did not use the word.

Once the distinction between a thing and its use or its way of affecting me is established, I can begin to appreciate things as this or that even when I am not actually using or enjoying them. I recognize the thing as usable or enjoyable; it is familiar to me, and has shown me how it can be taken. The action of "taking as" is still at work here, but it has been made internal. I still "take" things, but no longer with the hands or mouth. My mind, resting on the memories of what I have done, begins to "grasp" things, to "know" them. Most of the words we have to name our ability to recognize things originate metaphorically from words which name physical prehension, use, or enjoyment. Even "to know" is derived from a verb meaning "knowing how" or "can." This line of metaphorical development is not accidental; it reflects the gradual assimilation inward of bodily and public actions. And because both the internal and the external versions of the action involve a double vision, seeing the thing as this or that, the term "taking as" can be used to cover the two of them.

To say that we now take things internally does not mean that we begin to react to our ideas or images instead of reacting to things. We continue to deal with the same objects we earlier pushed around or tasted, but we refrain from any actual involvement with them here and now. We simply recognize them as soliciting our use or lending themselves to our pleasure, but for the moment we do no more than "perceive" them "as" employable or pleasant. If we slip from perception to the still more internal process of reverie or re-membering, we do start to entertain replicas of some sort in the place of things, but the element of "taking as" is still dominant. Imagination and memory involve ourselves as also imagined or remembered, as engaged in what we bring to mind; we represent ourselves as intervening in what is going on or as perceiving it with pleasure or pain. This is a still further level at which things can be "taken as" something or other.

Although we may have made our acceptance of things and their aspects internal in perception and imagination and memory, we still have not spoken. Even if we had formulated two names, one for the thing and one for its aspect, we would not have entered into language. The decisive change occurs when we move, by whatever grammatical device is available, from the action of "taking as" to "saying is." The double vision engendered by "taking as" now becomes sanctioned by using the copula "is." This is a transformation of the internalized version of "taking as"; we could not have moved directly from using a brick as a doorstop or enjoying mint as sweet to saying the brick is a doorstop and the mint is sweet. The internal "taking" is an intermediate step of detachment, a move away from using and enjoying things, which must be made before things can be registered as being in a certain way. The internal taking, whether in perception or reverie, is a passive acceptance that things *appear* in a certain way; the assertion with "is" is a claim that they *are* in such a way.

How do we move from "taking as" to "saying is"? Is the use of "is" simply a prolongation of the various stages of taking things as such and such? Does it bubble up, as a final stage, from use, enjoyment, perception, and reverie? No; the assertion with "is" enters from another direction. While I carry on the process of "taking as" and make it internal, I also hear other people speak, people who tell me this is hot, this is cold, this is sweet; to lift the cup, push the box, move my arm. I internalize this linguistic performance as well, and involve it with my process of "taking as." There is always an element of publicness in the linguistic performance, because I make internal what others are doing, and this dimension of "someone else" is never eliminated in speech; even when I speak to myself, I engender a minimal difference within me between speaker and audience. The absorption of language is something like the psychoanalytical superego to our perception, memory, and imagination. And the publicness of speech works in the outward direction also, because even when we say things to ourselves we are tentatively rehearsing the assertion as to be said for others; we describe things as they are to be found by anyone who will look at them.

To say an object is this or that is to perform an action. At first the incipient speaker is little more than an echo of other speakers; he repeats what they are saying, so that his voice is an appendage to theirs. Even at this stage, however, he is somewhat differentiated from the others because it is his physical voice, not theirs, that sounds under his control. As time goes on he becomes capable of reacting to things with assertions he initiates himself; this in turn makes it possible for him gradually to identify himself as someone who takes independent positions, and he begins to say "I." The "I" is the agent especially involved in the actions that generate the syntactical aspects of speech.

The assertion that an object is something or other is fused with our internalized "taking" of the object "as" such and such. The fusion or identification is a kind of repetition. The perceptual or imaginative "taking as" is a more passive procedure: we accept an object as having this or that aspect, we take the mint as sweet. Then we repeat this motion, distinguishing the object and its aspect, but we do it now with grammatical articulation. We say the mint is sweet. Moreover, we do not carry out these two processes side by side; what is presented in the second is experienced as "the same" as what had been given in the first. The same condition of the object—the object with this aspect—is there in both, with two important differences: it is now penetrated by the grammar made available in the language we speak, and it is explicitly guaranteed by us as speakers of the language and as perceivers who claim to have seen what condition the things are in. Husserl has described these two levels of judgment, and their fusion, in §50a of *Experience and Judgment*. He calls the passively engendered base the *Sachlage* and the actively constituted, grammatically saturated version the *Sachverhalt*.[1]

While we are finding our way about in the world, while we learn to take things in many different ways, we are also assimilating a language. The language not only caps what we have learned by experience, whether enjoyment or use; it also exercises a downward pressure on how we respond to things, and directs us to use them in certain ways and to perceive certain aspects of them. Most of the distinctions we make in things, even those brought about by what others tell us, are utilitarian, for employment, pleasure, or avoidance of pain. But once we have become accustomed to making distinctions, we may come to make them for their own sake, simply for the pleasure of knowing. We could not have started out with such disinterested distinctions, but they become possible on the foundation laid by utilitarian speech and experience.

The distinctions in things which are suggested by our language become the chief source for the aspects we notice; indeed there are many aspects we speak about which we never processed through the stages of being "taken as" in use, enjoyment, or perception. In discussing them we simply repeat what others say. What many people say about politics, for example, or science, may be like this. However, there are large areas of experience, especially those related to our immediate life, where we do have a base in use, enjoyment, and perception for what we say. Echoed speech, like counterfeit coin, is possible only because there is an authentic thing for which it can be mistaken. Strawson calls the subject-predicate structure the "basic combination" in logic;[2] it may be the most elementary structure for logic, which describes formal arrangements pervading all uses of language which involve truth, but it is possible to move to a "more basic combination" which supports predication: the distinction and unification between an object and its aspect engendered when we, in a prelinguistic way, "take" the object "as" something or other. "Is" is preceded by "as."[3]

Because this is so, grammatically structured linguistic statements are verified by the perceptions that underlie them. We have described perception as an internalized version of "taking" an object "as" this or that; it is not simply putting the object before us, it is taking it as having this or that aspect. The distinction of "as" is involved in perception. A predication is verified therefore not by matching it somehow with an undifferentiated object, but by allowing it to sink back to the pregrammatical distinction of object and aspect, whole and part, which we experience in perception. The statement is de-syntaxed, but the distinction in its lexical core remains in what we continue to experience and is seen to be identified with the fully articulated parts of the statement; the "as" is seen to be congruent with the "is" we have spoken. This is what occurs when we stop talking about things and look once again to see if they really are as we say.

The object and the aspect distinguished in our "taking as" are named by the lexical dimension of our speech, while the relationship they have to one another, their distinction and togetherness, their *synthesis* and *diairesis*, comes to expression in the syntactical dimension. Of course, this distinction and togetherness are not themselves objects, nor are they further aspects of the object— rather, they allow the object to have aspects—so they do not receive normal names from the lexicon; they must be expressed in syntax. Moreover, it is not the case that we first establish names and then add syntactical elements to them. Names and syntax come together when we enter into language, like melody and rhythm in music. The indifference to gratification and loss, confrontation and release, which naming gives is at the same time an appreciation of things which makes it possible for us to make statements about them. What we do with things when we become able to name them and their aspects is to talk about them. The detachment which naming provides is thus an invitation to a new way of treating things, by exploring them and saying what is true of them. We never name without at least an incipient combining of what we name.

The action of speaking about things, of distinguishing and unify-ing them with their aspects and disclosing what they are, is also detached in the sense that it does not modify what it speaks about. Speaking about things does not change them chemically, biologi-cally, or in any other way that would make us say different things about them while we describe them in our thing-directed dis-course. It merely allows them to be presented, to appear, to be truthful. Its only effect on the object is to manifest it and make it known. This is as it should be, for if the object were modified in a thing-like way by being known, if it received new features to be added to its customary predicates, we would never know the thing as it is itself, but only as it is affected by our knowledge. However, although being manifest and being known are not new features or new things, they are not nothing at all. They are occurrences in a different dimension. Activating the knowability or truthfulness of things is not doing nothing (although, as Heidegger suggests, it is "nothing" in the realm of customary features and things); it is what we do for things when we speak about them.[4] Truthfulness does not come forward as another thing, but it does emerge as an element in being. Only if we limit being to things, and permit no differences except those among things and the attributes of things, will we have to say that truthfulness does not exist.

As we have seen in chapter two, verbs name a manifestation of the subject, and the manifestation may occur either as a simple attribute or as an action the subject is engaged in. The "basic combination" of predication, therefore, is the fusion of a subject and a way in which it manifests itself. In the prepredicative action of "taking as," we also deal with manifestations of the thing we are taking. Using an object or allowing it to affect us is to provoke it to display itself, to show what possibilities it has. By using a brick as a doorstop we disclose a "doorstoppy" quality in it: resistant, solid, unmovable, massive. As we use things in many ways and let them affect us diversely, we gradually invest the thing with many ways it can be taken, and the thing becomes identifiable as the same thing, the identity, in all these manifestations. The procedure of "taking as" is obviously more aggressive, more provocative of distinctions between thing and aspect or appearance, than is the action of predicating, which assumes the distinctions have been made and sanctions them as being "real" appearances and not just coincidences.

We have observed that when someone is engaged in "taking" an object as this or that, he does not use the word "as"; he need not use any words at all. The term "taking as" is used by us when we analyze, philosophically, what he is doing. However, if he predicates, he does use the word "is" or the equivalent which his language provides; the predication may be expressed merely by the way the names are conjoined, but it does find expression. The speaker uses a syntactic word or element in his speech. This is an indication of his explicit activity in predicating, a sign that he takes a position and authorizes what he says to be the case. As we showed in chapter one, the syntax of language becomes more and more important as we take greater responsibility for what we say, as we move from evocation to registration to reporting; and it is less important to the degree that we use words rather to suggest aspects of things as they appear before us. Even in the latter case, however, in evocation, for example, or in enhancing a perception we share with others, the syntactical aspect is not annihilated but only becomes extremely vague and indifferent. Any use of words involves at least an incipient syntax.

Logicians have shown that in determining the logical validity of statements, very few logical particles suffice in the syntax of formal languages: signs for predication, quantification, negation, and conjunction, for example, may be enough, and all other logical operations may be reduced to these in determining truth values. This may be the case if our only concern with language is logical consistency and, subsequently, the truth we determine by verification; we take into account merely the statement and the condition of the object expressed in the statement. However, in the actual use of language we must also consider the addressee: the speech is spoken to someone. This dimension allows a luxurious proliferation of syntax, because part of the speaker's syntactical performance is governed by how he wishes the listener to take what he is saying. The speaker feints and jostles with his interlocutor. For example, if he joins two parts of his speech by "but" or "nevertheless," he implies that the first part arouses a certain expectation in his addressee, then he cancels this expectation by what he says in the second part: "They all went home, but Peter remained"; "They found the house pleasant; nevertheless they did not stay." As far as logic or verification goes, both of these complex statements might as well have used the simple conjunction "and." The truth tables for "and" would suffice for "but" or "nevertheless," and the latter could be melted down, logically, to the former, but such a reduction would eliminate part of the sense of these conjunctions, the part that works in the moves made between the speaker and his audience.[5] Other conjunctions may have the sense of concession, emphatic addition, comparison, restriction, indifference, parallelism, and the like, all of which could be bleached into the neutral "and" for the purposes of logic and simple truth. Because such composition takes into account the mind of the addressee and tries to make the statement persuasive for him, it would not be out of place to speak of the rhetorical aspect in syntax.

However, the rhetorical aspect of syntax is quite different from what Aristotle describes as the function of rhetoric. The rhetoric he analyzes is on a more complex level of discourse than what we are discussing: in Aristotelian rhetoric we make a speech in order to persuade others to perform a certain action or pass a certain law, to decide a certain judicial case in a particular way, or to adopt a certain attitude and belief toward some person, thing, or event. In all such cases of rhetoric, legal, practical, judicial, or epideictic, our speech aims at bringing about something that is beyond the speech itself; the audience is persuaded to do something or to adopt an attitude. In the rhetoric of syntax we deal with something much more intimate: the speaker wishes merely to make the addressee follow the speech, to perform the syntactical operations along with him, to let, in effect, the speech take place. This must be achieved before any subsequent action following from the discourse can be accomplished. The speaker at this point wants his audience only to give him their minds and lend him their ears.

The speaker carries out syntactical operations while he speaks; he combines and separates names in diverse ways, according to the possibilities his language gives. His syntactical performances are carried out upon the base of his own sounding voice, like motions made by a surfer riding a wave. The listener, however, does not himself repeat the voice of the speaker; he carries out his syntactical moves upon the voice he is hearing. There is only one sounding speech, but two executions: the speaker's performance of syntax is the commanding, guiding one; the listener's performance is led by the other, but he too must execute and perform the syntax, in his apprenticed way, or there will be no speech. "Speech is creative from the speaker's standpoint, but he has not *spoken* at all if he has not been understood."[6] And understanding means primarily the actual execution of syntactical moves on the basis of someone else's voice. We must add to this the fact that the speaker himself has to overhear his own voice sounding, to listen marginally to his own speech as he controls it syntactically; if he could not do so he would be unable to compose speech wholes, and would lapse into babbling or silence.

Notes

1. Edmund Husserl, *Experience and Judgment: Investigations in a Genealogy of Logic*, ed. L. Landgrebe, trans. J. S. Churchill and K. Ameriks (Evanston: Northwestern University Press, 1973).

2. Peter Strawson, *Subject and Predicate in Logic and Grammar* (London: Methuen, 1974), p. 4.

3. Heidegger speaks of the "hermeneutical 'as'" as supporting the "apophantical 'as'" of an assertion; we express the former as "taking as." See *Being and Time*, trans. J. Macquarrie and E. Robinson (New York: Harper and Row, 1962), §33; also *Logik: Die Frage nach der Wahrheit*, Collected Works, vol. 21 (Frankfurt: Klostermann, 1976), §12.

4. Martin Heidegger, *Die Grundprobleme der Phänomenologie*, Collected Works, vol. 24, p. 304: "Dann lässt sich zeigen, wie die Wahrheit nichts Seiendes ist, das under anderen vorhandenen Dingen vorkommt." All of §18 is relevant to this topic. See also *Zur Sache des Denkens* (Tübingen: Niemeyer, 1969), p. 3; also Edmund Husserl, *Logical Investigations*, trans. J. N. Findlay (New York: Humanities Press, 1970), Investigation VI, §43-§44.

5. Cf. Michael Dummett, *Frege: Philosophy of Language* (London: Duckworth, 1973), pp. 2-3, 83-89.

6. William J. Entwistle, *Aspects of Language* (London: Faber and Faber, 1953), p. 50.

CHAPTER 6

Complications of Syntax in Four Directions. The Proposition

We perform activities when we achieve the syntax of a sentence. The basic combination of subject and predicate is the most elementary part of syntax, and the activity of predicating is the most elementary kind of syntactical performance. But many other kinds of performance are possible, constituting many other syntactical forms. They arise because of complexities which are possible along three different directions. First, the object and manifestation named in the sentence can be articulated in a more expanded way: we may add adjectives, conjunctives, adverbs, prepositions, further noun cases, and tenses and moods. Secondly, we can make more intricate the rhetorical aspect of syntax, evolving the sentence or the chain of sentences in more complex and perhaps more pleasing ways. Thirdly, we can nominalize, as a whole, the object with its aspect, and allow it to enter into more complex arrangements.

Let us discuss the third of these possibilities. When we nominalize a fact, an object as manifested in a certain way, we give it a name.[1] We do to the arrangement of thing-with-aspect what we previously did to the thing and the aspect separately. Then, as is to be expected, we work syntax upon the fact we have named, and make it enter, as a whole, into a more complex fact. The words we use to name the fact are very often complex: "That Peter arrived late was lucky." We could also have called the fact "Peter's late arrival," or perhaps something else. It is, incidentally, interesting that the conjunction "that," in "that Peter arrived late," was originally a demonstrative, with the sense: "This: Peter arrived late, was lucky." In Greek, the conjunction *hoti* evolved from the demonstrative *ho*, and in Latin *quod* developed from the relative pronoun, which also has a demonstrative sense. These grammatical evolutions confirm the claim that when we utter a phrase like "that he came late," we name the fact. We no longer articulate the fact when we say these words; rather, we stand back and, as it were, point to it or name it. Of course, instead of the complex name, we could use the simple pronoun for the fact and say "That was lucky." When we name the object's having an aspect, we compress what we once articulated so that we can carry on another articulation—not directly on the same subject which served in the first articulation, but on the whole fact.

When we nominalize a fact we do not turn away from things and name our ideas, judgments, images, or anything else in our minds. We name things with their aspects, and our names are just as world-directed as when we name trees and rivers. But we name things as they have been articulated by us, as they have manifested themselves to us. The process of nominalizing can be iterated: we can name not just a first-level fact with a material thing as subject, but also the facts which have as their subjects other nominalized facts. This can go on indefinitely. In the reverse direction, we can unpack higher-level facts into their ingredient facts, until we come down to the objects and aspects at their base. These in turn can be allowed to recede beyond syntax, as we move down into the perceptual "taking as" that underlies all syntactic structure. On all these levels, however, there is no change of direction: our syntactic actions continue to be carried out on things and facts, and our names continue to name things and facts, never something "subjective." There is, of course, a point at which we turn from facts and things to our judgments, but it is not reached when we nominalize facts.

The perceptual "taking as" underlies first-level facts and their syntax. Is there a role for "taking as" when we move from first-level to second-level facts, from "Peter arrived late" to "Peter's late arrival was lucky"? Yes, there is. The object "taken as" something or other allows complications. For example, once I have invested a certain usefulness or affection in an object—even if I have not yet formulated any syntax for it—this investment remains as a deposit in the object, and I can discover still more aspects in it as I use or enjoy it further. I have used a brick as a doorstop; it has a "doorstoppy" deposit. I find by chance that it sinks in water; it then acquires this sense too. I can go on indefinitely like this as the object gets more familiar to me. But in these cases I merely add more and more manifestations and deposits, all on the same level. I can also build upon one of the deposits: after seeing, for example, that the brick in question, because of its material, decomposes in water, I may try to keep it in a dry area. This new investment of sense, to be kept dry, is not simply added to the brick; it is added to the brick as decomposable in water. We have the following arrangement: (brick taken as decomposable in water) taken as to be kept dry. This building up of "taking as," one upon the other, can be done through many levels without syntax.

Now when we do involve syntax, the higher-level fact is not limited to the actual grammar of the lower-level fact. All it needs as its ingredient is what Husserl calls the *Sachlage*, the condition of the object, the object-with-aspect, not any particular grammar that might shape the arrangement.[2] "Peter/coming late" is the important ingredient, whether we say "Peter's coming late" or "Peter's late arrival" or "that Peter came late" as the subject for "was lucky." Therefore there is a "taking as" at work between first- and second-level facts, between second- and third-level facts, and so on. This means that the articulated fact on one level has to become digested before it can become an ingredient for a higher level; it has to become something we can hold together independently of the particular grammar in which it has been packaged for us. We have to get used to the fact, it has to become familiar to us, slipped back into the state of being "taken as" instead of being "said to be." Unless we acquire this flexibility with the fact, we cannot think about it, make it an ingredient of a higher level. It may be hard for us to do so; we may be holding on to the fact primarily on the authority of someone else, clinging to its syntax as it has been given to us because we do not trust ourselves to let go, to say it in other terms. For the time being at least we do not really understand the combination of names we express. Think, for example, of a physics student barely able to follow a certain experiment, and being very uncertain about integrating it into higher-level relationships, laws, and facts. But when his grasp on the experiment becomes less rigid, when what happens in it becomes more familiar to him, moving on to higher stages is no problem.

It might appear that names of objects are also, implicitly, names of compressed facts. If I name Dwight Eisenhower or my car, I imply in what I name the deposit of certain facts I know about it: Eisenhower was commander of Allied forces in Europe during the Second World War, and my car has a dented fender. Some such facts are, of course, relative to the person who uses the name: someone who knew Eisenhower only as a young man would not imply his being commander when he used the name. However, other facts, those we might call the essentials of the object, may be implied by all who name it: Eisenhower was born of human parents, could speak and laugh, had a memory; my car moves from place to place and carries passengers. It would appear that practically all names have some such essential connotations, some such necessities, except perhaps the rudimentary kind of name we find in exclamations, when the speaker merely alerts others to something prominent. Shall we say that names name such implied essential facts, and perhaps some of the contingent facts in which the named object has become involved?

There is some truth to this proposal. We are never faced with a totally unfamiliar object, one that is acquiring its absolutely first aspect for us. If we have progressed so far as to begin distinguishing an object from its aspect or manifestations—that is, if we have gone beyond the continuous experience of masses, moods, and states which find expression in the gerundial level of speech—we must have acquired some familiarity with the object in question. The stone that we find can be used as a doorstop is also, most probably, the stone that was rather heavy for us to carry. Nothing appears to us as an absolutely undifferentiated object, if it is an object at all. Every name seems to connote some facts, and perhaps some necessary facts, about what it names, facts that can be unpacked in what we commonly call the definition of the thing named.

Nevertheless, it would be wrong to say that the name of the object is also the name of these facts; to do so would overlook an important distinction. When we use the object's name, we do not nominalize any of the thing's essentials; when we do nominalize them, we take a further step. We do something we have not done before. If the name served to name all the essential facts as well as the object, we would never need to make the essentials explicit. But as we shall see in our treatment of essentials, this is often necessary. It is best, then, to keep the distinction between naming an object and naming a fact, even while admitting that the object named may contain the deposit of many facts; they still have not explicitly been named.

At the beginning of this chapter we listed three ways in which syntax can become elaborated: in articulating the various aspects or manifestations of things; in its rhetorical devices to solicit the performances of the addressee; in the nominalization of facts. We must now add a fourth: besides dealing with objects, facts, or the audience of the speech, we can also refer to the persons—the speakers or potential speakers—who do or do not "have" the facts. We can speak of the registrars, reporters, namers, the performers of syntactic operations, or those who fail to know or "con" the facts. To move into this direction is not just to add more facts to those we have; it is to speak about the having of facts, and about the cognitive agents who bring about the facts. This dimension should not be flattened out into being just another set of added facts. If I say, for example, "John told me the house was on fire," or "John saw the house was on fire," I am not merely adding more facts about the burning building, as I might by saying, "The house was on fire; but it was insured; it burned for two hours." With my move into registrars and reporters of facts, I enter into the domain of quotation, persuasion, attribution, and the other possibilities that exist specifically among the speakers of language. New names become necessary, as well as a new dimension and complication of syntax. The new dimension could not arise without the nominalization of facts, but it is not just a further articulation of them. It begins to speak about the "owners" of the facts, those responsible for framing them.

The various devices for quotation allow us to state a fact not in our own voice, but as merely repeating someone else. The fact is taken not directly as mine, but as registered or reported by another. In this regard it is worth noting that the conjunction "that" which introduces many phrases in indirect discourse was also originally a demonstrative: "Lawrence said that the train was warm" meant, at the beginning, "Lawrence said this: the train was warm." Once again, a similar development occurred in Latin and Greek. It is clear that in such statements we nominalize a fact, and mention the speaker or perceiver who is responsible for registering or reporting it.

This possibility of language permits enormous complexity, especially in writing. Consider the following sentence from Henry James's *The Bostonians* (chapter 32): "This description of Verena was of course perfectly correct; but it was not agreeable to Olive to have the fact in question so clearly perceived, even by a person who expressed it with an air intimating that there was nothing in the world *she* couldn't understand." Almost all the words in this sentence name a compressed fact and the reaction of different fact-registrars or fact-reporters to it. (1) "This description" names the earlier articulation of a fact, which was narrated in the previous paragraph of the story, and the description is confirmed as accurate. (2) "The fact in question" names the crucial state of affairs revealed in the description. (3) This fact has been "clearly perceived" by someone. The registration of the fact is named, but the person who perceives it is identified, in this sentence, only as the registrar of the fact. (4) This perception is "not agreeable to Olive": she reacts not to the fact but to the perception of it, and so holds in mind both the fact and the other person's registration of it. (5) After the concessive conjunction "even," we are told that the perceiver of the fact also "expressed it" (the fact) with a certain air, intimating the inescapability of all facts before her perceptive powers. This ziggurat of relationships, so typical of James, is constructed upon the nominalized fact, and all the other names in the sentence, except those of Olive and Verena, name either the compressed fact or the syntactical performances or abilities of minds that know it. (Incidentally, it is necessary to include a proper name like "Olive" somewhere in such discourse, otherwise we would not be able to identify the facts in question. Some speaker or observer has to be mentioned at some point.)

Once we begin to take certain facts as discovered or reported by others, we also begin to identify the speakers who are responsible for them. The other person has already been identified as a spatiotemporal, physical, living object, and as an agent who has done certain things; he has already been addressed as an audience for my speaking; but now he becomes identifiable on a higher level, as someone who can also speak to me with a certain authority about things and their arrangements. He becomes capable of naming things and exercising syntax, the articulator of certain facts which might not have been realized had he not perceived, thought, and spoken. He becomes quotable, a participant in conversation. New forms of names and syntax are now needed to speak of him and others as seeing, thinking, knowing, saying, and the like.

We now have four avenues of complication in syntax: the articulation of things and their manifestations; the rhetorical aspect of syntax; nominalization of facts; indirect discourse and the attribution of facts to other speakers. None of these is reducible to any other. We must explore more fully the nature of syntax and syntactic action, but before doing so we will examine another theme: the distinction between a fact and its corresponding proposition, judgment, statement, opinion, supposition, or whatever it is to be called. We have not made this distinction so far in this chapter; we have only spoken about things and their aspects, facts articulated and nominalized, and about other people knowing them. The issue we raise now concerns the problem of truth, for we are to distinguish what it is that facts verify or confirm, what it is that matches or corresponds to facts. The problem of truth cannot be adequately treated if the nature of propositions is not properly understood. Furthermore, to explain the condition of other speakers who register or report facts—the fourth complication of syntax examined in this chapter—we must clarify what propositions are.

In determining the status of propositions, the position we wish to criticize and use as a foil takes the proposition as an entity which is somehow part of the psychological being of the person who holds it.[3] According to this opinion, the constituent parts of the proposition, concepts, are also parts of the knower's reality. Concepts and propositions are said to be a special kind of accident inhering in the substance of the one who has them; they may be a certain kind of sign, or image, or species, or expression, but they are said to be entities existing in the knower's substance. Since a proposition is considered to be a combination of concepts, the problem of truth is

to determine whether the judgmental composition matches a composition of substance and attributes in things. Here the combination of concepts, there the combination of object and features: how
can one be said to match the other? Our procedure will not be to
devise new and better ways of getting from concepts and propositions to reality; we will ask whether concepts and propositions
should be considered as entities in the knower in any sense at all.
The problem of trying to get "through" concepts and judgments
"to" things is a false problem, because concepts and propositions
do not exist in the way this position claims that they do; there is, in
fact, nothing that we have to get through or around to get to things.

Consider two speakers, Philip and Justin. Philip makes a statement about something: "This tree has the blight." Under normal
circumstances Justin also performs the syntax of this sentence and
considers the tree as being blighted. Both Justin and Philip work,
cognitively, on the tree. Both have together articulated the same
fact, one leading and the other following. However, it is always
possible for Justin to be less cooperative: he may perform the syntax of the sentence uttered by Philip, but may "take" what he says
not as a fact but only "as supposed" by Philip. In doing this he
modifies what he would spontaneously achieve. Instead of co-
registering a fact, he takes the fact as only a proposed fact, one put
forward by Philip. He distinguishes between a fact and a proposed
fact.

This distinction is related to different performances on Justin's
part. When Justin simply accepts what Philip says, he registers the
fact almost—but not quite—as if he himself were responding to a
perceptually taken situation. When he takes it as supposed, he adjusts the fact, he adds something to it. Imagine that Justin first went
along with Philip, but then looked more closely at the tree and saw
it did not have the blight. If Philip kept insisting on what he said,
Justin would still be dealing with the fact that the tree is blighted,
but he would take that fact as only proposed by Philip. Justin could
do this, incidentally, even if the tree did have the blight; he could
take the same fact simply as proposed by his interlocutor. A "real"
fact can also be turned into a supposition.

The important point here is that Justin does not refer to an accident in Philip when he refers to "what you said" or "your statement
or proposition or proposal" or "that the tree is blighted." Justin

continues to be tree-directed, but now makes the curious maneuver of taking this particular articulation of the tree as only proposed by Philip. What Justin does is very complex. He actually co-performs the syntax of the statement but adds an interpretation of "taking as" to the fact he achieves: the fact is "taken as supposed" by Philip.

Also, it is not true that Justin first generates judgments or propositions in his mind and then acquires access to things. He is with things, with the tree and its features, from the start. He first articulates the tree; the judgment, as a modification of a fact, comes later. The entire judgmental domain comes later, as a transformation of the domain of simple fact. Once we get used to the distinction between fact and judgment (fact as proposed), we become tempted to postulate the judgment as the original domain, the one we first achieve and the one closest to us, and we try to see the fact as what we reach in a derived way. But this is a philosophical construction which reverses the true order of things and turns "facts as proposed" into entities that have at least the subsistence of accidents in the mind. The problem of getting back to things and facts is not a difficulty arising in the nature of things; it is an artificial problem raised by misleading philosophical constructs.

Another way of formulating the difference between fact and proposition is to say that in registering or reporting a fact we articulate the fact and also assent to it, while in entertaining a proposal we articulate but withhold assent. This formulation can also be misleading: it implies that there are two distinct components, articulation and assent, and that the second can be subtracted, leaving the first by itself. But we do not subtract or withhold assent, we annul it. Turning a fact into a proposition is a positive achievement, a modification, not the removal of an element. Also, at the beginning, the articulation in question is not something merely related to assent, it is internally characterized by it; the kind of thing we are doing is assenting articulatedly or articulating assentedly; such articulation exists only as shot through with belief.[4] Then we adjust this naive registration or report. We transform it into a "mere" articulation or proposal. But this is a transformation, not the uncovering of something that was concealed in our achievement all along. It is philosophically incorrect to project the proposition, the result of a modification, into the situation that precedes its emergence.

Also, it is clear that turning a fact into a fact as supposed is quite different from nominalizing a fact. Nominalization is a modification of the articulation of the fact; we collapse the fact and make it ingredient into a new fact, but in doing this we do not modify the assent that characterized our original report or registration. The fact remains permeated with belief as we go on to incorporate it into new articulations; it does not become a proposition. If we use the terms "articulation/assent" carefully, we can say that nominalization compresses the articulated but sustains assent, while turning a fact into a proposition keeps the articulation but suppresses assent.

It takes a certain refinement to distinguish between a fact and a proposition, to carry out the syntactical articulation while inhibiting assent. At the beginning, we go along with whatever we hear being said. Even when we begin to distinguish between fact and proposal, the syntactical articulation that we must continue to perform while we entertain something as supposed pulls along with itself a tendency to assent. The rhetorical force of the syntax continues to work on us, and we must remain cool in resisting it. Besides intellectual expertness in distinguishing fact and fact as supposed, a certain emotional control is required to tolerate a proposition as only a supposition. When listening to what someone says, we will always feel some sense of being pushed to admit the facts as the speaker frames them. People sometimes feel contaminated by statements they hear even though they do not agree with them; they may not admit the truth of these propositions, but the mere articulation they must perform in hearing them seems to make the hearers also assent in ever so slight a degree. This kind of response may depend on the issues being discussed and the emotional state of the speaker and listener at the moment, and it explains in part why some people, even when they do not agree, can become very hostile to others who assert unpleasant things.

In saying that a proposition is a supposed fact taken as supposed, we again use the term "taking as," which we have encountered in several earlier analyses. In particular: (1) in predicative experience we take an object as soft or sinkable; (2) in nominalization we take a condensed fact as ingredient in higher-level facts. These two cases, however, have nothing to do with the supposed as supposed, because they lead on to the articulation of new features and predicates in the objects under discussion. However, (3) we can relate a fact to the persons who "have" the fact, to the registrars, reporters, perceivers, namers, speakers, and the rest ("Peter saw the house burn down"); we take the fact "as possessed" in some way by such persons. This dimension has been discussed earlier in this chapter, and it is associated with our present theme of taking the supposed as supposed. The very domain of speakers, registrars, and reporters arises along with the emergence of the propositional, for only when positions and truths can be attributed can a community of speakers be established.

Furthermore, we can not only turn a fact that someone else reports into a proposition; we can do the same to what we say ourselves. This is the example Husserl uses in *Formal and Transcendental Logic* (§44), where he presents the position we have developed here.[5] If we articulate a certain fact and later find that we were wrong in asserting it, we can still entertain the same fact, but only as once proposed or supposed by us. In such a case we take beliefs we once had—and not the proposals others make—as "mere" opinions. And once the propositional domain has been distinguished from the domain of fact, we can turn convictions that we have not rejected, facts we still believe, into propositions, for the sake of testing them more thoroughly against what we find to be the case. The emergence of the propositional allows us to take a distance to our own convictions.

The supposed fact as supposed is what we call the proposition, judgment, statement, opinion, or supposition. In this chapter we have tried to describe the status of propositions, chiefly by drawing contrasts with a theory that takes propositions and concepts to be accidental entities in the knower. We have not yet explained what propositions are in themselves, and why and how facts can be transformed in this remarkable way into the supposed as supposed. We will continue to investigate this issue.

Notes

1. On "nominalizing" see Edmund Husserl, *Formal and Transcendental Logic*, trans. D. Cairns (The Hague: Nijhoff, 1969), § 42; also *Logical In-*

vestigations, trans. J. N. Findlay (New York: Humanities Press, 1970), Investigation IV, §11; Investigation V, §37-§38.

2. See above, p. 44.

3. This position has origins at least as far back as the Middle Ages and may reach back to the Stoics. For an exposition of its medieval formulation, see John F. Peifer, *The Mystery of Knowledge* (Albany: Magi Books, 1964), esp. pp. 132-212; this book was originally published under the title, *The Concept in Thomism.* See also Yves Simon, *Introduction à l'ontologie du connaître* (Paris: Desclée De Brouwer, 1934; reprinted Dubuque: Brown Reprint Co., n.d.), pp. 19-27. The Scholastics had to postulate what they called an "expressed intellectual species" or a "formal concept" or the "inner word," "because the intellect understands indifferently an absent thing and a present thing" (citation from St. Thomas on p. 139 of Peifer). However, this formal concept has to be qualified in many ways, and is described as a most unusual kind of sign. My treatment of the proposition is an attempt to handle the problems of presence and absence, and to account for the phenomena the Scholastic "formal concept" is supposed to explain, while avoiding the inconveniences of postulating this special kind of sign. The doctrine of something like a formal concept has influenced the epistemologies and metaphysics of philosophers since the Middle Ages, and is still at work in such issues as Frege's realm of "thoughts" and in the controversy whether propositions should be posited as distinct from sentences. Husserl's notion of intentionality provides the first way of coming to terms with the problem. Incidentally, the Scholastic notion of "concept" is not found in Aristotle; see Martin Heidegger, *Logik: Die Frage nach der Wahrheit,* Collected Works, vol. 21 (Frankfurt: Klostermann, 1976), pp. 166-67.

4. The separation of articulation from assent is criticized by Heidegger, who uses Lotze's formulation as his foil; see *Die Grundprobleme der Phänomenologie,* Collected Works, vol. 24 (Frankfurt: Klostermann, 1976), pp. 282-85. He goes on to call judgment an "aufzeigendes Auseinanderlegen" (p. 298). Heidegger here develops a notion of judgment already found in Husserl's *Logical Investigations.* See also Gilbert Ryle, *The Concept of Mind* (London: Hutchinson, 1949), p. 264: "Logicians and epistemologists sometimes assume, what I for a long time assumed, that entertaining a proposition is a more elementary or naive performance than affirming that something is the case. . . . This is a mistake. The concept of make-believe is of a higher order than that of belief."

5. For an analysis of these themes in *Formal and Transcendental Logic,* see Robert Sokolowski, *Husserlian Meditations: How Words Present Things* (Evanston: Northwestern University Press, 1974), pp. 43-54, 275-82.

CHAPTER 7

Words and Sentences as Achievements

We have contrasted propositions with facts to make an initial definition of them: propositions are facts taken as supposed. But by denying that propositions are psychological entities, we seem to be left with nothing to which they can be attached. If propositions are not somehow "in the mind," as signs perhaps, where can they be? We turn to words and sentences as the place where we are to locate them. But propositions are not simply equivalent to sentences, and it is in showing how the two are related and distinguished that we will further define what a proposition is. What we shall determine in this way will explain why the proposition is a fact taken as supposed.

There is an erroneous way to explain how a word is present to us. It is sometimes said that we are given, perceptually, certain sounds or marks, and that we impose a category upon them, just as we might apply the category "umbrella" to the thin, black shape we perceive in the corner. According to this opinion, we would apply the category "the word 'house'" to the written or spoken marks or sounds h-o-u-s-e. But this is not how we perceive words; they are not like ordinary perceptual objects which we recognize. Instead, we must achieve the word for it to be present to us. We react to the marks or sounds h-o-u-s-e by making the word "house," by executing it, not by applying a category. After we have made the word, it is possible for us to apply concepts to it and say that this is the word "house," or that this is a noun, or a commonly used English word.

But what we apply such concepts to is the thing we have brought about by our linguistic achievement, not certain sensuous givens. It is not like calling a green mass a curtain, or a white expanse a cloud. Thus when we classify words grammatically, we do a double linguistic duty: we speak about words which have already been spoken as words.

A similar achievement must intervene in presenting the written letters of a word. If I see the mark *t*, then the mark *h*, then *e*, I do not apply the concepts "the letter 't'," "the letter 'h'," "the letter 'e'" to them and so have the word "the." Rather, I execute the letters; I say them. Only after I have made them can I look back at them and say, "This is the letter 't' and this is the letter 'h'." Until I have made them they are not there. If we deal with speech instead of writing, a similar condition holds. Here someone else says the parts of the word, he makes the sounds as phonemes, and I make them along with him while I listen; but only after we have executed the sounds as phonemes in this extraordinary double agency, one leading and the other following, can we look back and speak of the phonemes that are there.

There is one kind of concept that may have to be applied to marks or sounds before our performance takes place: we must first take them as writing or as speech in order to be aware that our execution is being solicited. We must know these marks are not arabesques or random scratches, that these noises are not grunts or moans or babbling. Often enough the categories of written or spoken speech are applied even when we cannot achieve the letters, phonemes, and words because we do not know the language, but such an achievement is what we are called upon to do.

A letter, a phoneme, or a word is an achievement in the double sense of the term: it involves an achieving, an activity performed by the reader or speaker, and it involves something achieved, a product. The execution of language is a cross between *praxis* and *poiēsis*, doing and making. It is like making because it engenders a product distinct from the process of making; the letter or phoneme or word is more than the process of uttering it. In this respect producing the word "lamplight" is like the carpenter's production of a table. However, the carpenter's table remains when the carpenter stops making it, and remains even when he leaves the scene entirely. But the word and its parts only come into actual being while they are being executed; someone has to be doing the word for it actually to exist. In this respect speech is more like *praxis*, like an exercise of judiciousness or temperance or generosity, which exist only in their performance. The word is never identified with the act that makes it, but it does cease to actually exist when the act ends. This ambiguous condition of words and their parts is not to be resolved either by reducing them to actions and denying that they are identifiable as anything beyond the performance, or by giving them an existence independent of any performance by a speaker.

When no one is saying the word "lamplight," it falls into a kind of latent existence; but when it is said again by someone, it returns as the very same word that was said before by him or by another speaker. It is not a similar word, but the same one. This is why the word and its parts are said to be products distinguishable from the activities that bring them about, for when we repeat an activity we have a performance which is only similar to, and not identical with, the previous performance. These similar activities achieve the same word. Likewise, if someone else speaks and I listen, each performs his own psychological act, but the same word is achieved by both of us: there is only one "lamplight" being made by two agents. The word must therefore be distinguished from the activities each of us carries out.

Reading or hearing words is an elusive achievement because it does not change in any perceivable way the marks or sounds that occasion the performance. We do not make the letters thicker or brighter when we read, we do not make the sounds louder when we understand what someone is saying. It would appear that nothing real has been done. The only change is that the marks and sounds are now "read words" or "understood words"; the marks and sounds are activated as words. This is not a difference that a physicist could discriminate in the marks and sounds, but it is a difference nonetheless, a difference that establishes the object which the linguist or the grammarian studies. And while the grammarian examines the object brought about in this difference, the philosopher examines the difference itself, as well as the performance that brings it about. The grammarian takes the presence of the words for granted, the philosopher describes how their presence has come to pass. It is this kind of difference—like that between marks and read words, one that does not change physically the sensuous object it deals with—that will be at work between sentences and propositions, and between propositions and facts.

Where is the written and read word? On the page. Where is the spoken word which I hear and comprehend? In the scope of my hearing, as far as the speaker's voice can be heard. The word is where its letters or phonemes are, and they are where the marks and sounds are, just as my salute is where my hand is. The word is wherever its ingredients are; it is not a sign in my psyche or in my imagination. The word is public and has a physical component. If I happen to be "speaking internally," then the words are wherever my imagination is, but in the normal condition of speech, publicly expressed, the word is wherever its sounds and marks are. Similarly, a fact is wherever its ingredients are—its trees and tables and lizards—and a proposition is wherever its sentence may be.

Although phonemes have to be achieved, there is a difference in the way the two species of phonemes, consonants and vowels, are made. They are not simply juxtaposed; rather, vowels are presupposed by consonants and serve as a foundation for them. The etymology of "consonant" itself suggests this: it "sounds with" another sound. Besides being subordinated to the vowel by having less sonority, the consonant also works on the vowel. Consonants clip the continuous vowel sound. In this respect the consonant is to the vowel as the syntax of a sentence is to its lexicon. It is more a positive performance carried out on something that is given beforehand as its condition. True, the vowel involves a certain activity and selection of sound, but this kind of action becomes passive in respect to the greater activity of the consonant executed on the vowel. The more prominent making of the word consists in the consonantal clips. Consequently, no alphabetic writing can afford to exclude consonants—those essential instructions for the manufacture of a word—but some languages do omit vowels. As David Diringer observes, "It is simply incorrect to assume that a written script whose particular economy is the non-representation of vowels poses any particular difficulty for those accustomed to reading it, and a smpl tst 'f ths srt shld shw ths qut wll."[1] On the other hand, it is impossible to omit vowels when we speak; they come first as the element of the voice, they are the bellowing part of speech while consonants are the clips, cuts, trims, and interruptions that shape the continuous column of sound. In speaking, both consonants and vowels are indispensable.

The vowel sound is a continuum. If we utter a long, uninterrupted "a" sound, it is impossible for us to say how many "a's" we are making, impossible to determine when one ends and another begins. Furthermore, if the sound is stopped and started again, it is impossible to tell whether the new sound is a continuation of the old or a repetition of it. A continuum is precisely the kind of thing in which these distinctions—between definite units, and between continuation and repetition—cannot be made. But the consonant breaks up the vowel continuum upon which it is carried out. It is punctual. The "t" in the Latin word *"ita"* is a single performance that puts an edge on the vowels "i" and "a" in this word; and when combined with the other boundaries of silence before and after the word, it indicates that there is only one vowel before and one after the consonant, no matter how long they may be drawn out.

In addition, there is never any problem determining whether a consonant is a continuation of an earlier one, or a repetition, a new instance of it: because they are punctual clips, no consonant is continuous with an earlier one; each is a new performance of the particular phoneme, a repetition of what was done before. Each time a "p" or a "t" or a "b" is uttered, the consonantal phoneme is repeated anew; it is discrete, not continuous. This individuating, punctuating, discrete force of the consonant is carried over into the production of words and individuates instances of them also. If I say the word "irate" two times, I have a repetition of the same word, not a continuation of the one word, and it is the consonants that bring this possibility of repetition about. The vowel sounds by themselves, with their continuous wail, would not allow me to distinguish whether I have two instances of the same word, or only one long word.

A completely new kind of activity arises when a child begins to select phonemes; there is a qualitative change from the prelinguistic period. In the prelinguistic period the child revels in a whole jungle of sounds, none of which is ever chosen explicitly as individually "the same sound" again; there are only similar sounds or continuations of a sound. As Roman Jakobson writes, "The actual beginning stages of language, as is known, are preceded by the so-called babbling period, which brings to light in many children an astonishing quantity and diversity of sound productions. A child, during his babbling period, can accumulate articulations which are never found within a single language or even a group of languages—consonants of any place of articulation, palatized and rounded consonants, sibilants, affricates, clicks, complex vowels, diphthongs, etc." It has been said that at this stage the child can execute any conceivable sound. However, Jakobson continues, "As all observers acknowledge with great surprise, the child then loses nearly all of his ability to produce sounds in passing over from the pre-language stage to the first acquisition of words, i.e. to the first genuine stage of language." Even sounds he will later need, and which others around him use, are lost: "Indeed, the child is generally successful in recovering these sounds only after long effort, sometimes only after several years."[2] Sounds that were once babbled now have to be chosen as phonemes, and the two ways of making them are radically different.

As elementary as it might be, there is a new sense of identity which arises with the achievement of phonemes, especially the achievement of consonants, which are clearly repeated as the same thing each time they are made. On this rudimentary level, the speaker becomes aware of having exactly the same item again, not merely a similar item, nor a continuation of an earlier one, but a break with what is going on and an explicit return to "the same again." This sense of having exactly the same thing repeated is not found in any activity, experience, or object before consonants arise; it is in turn the basis for higher-level identities, such as words or sentences, with their explicit beginnings and ends. It is also the basis for our ability to perceive an object as identically the same as the one we saw before. This is related to our ability to distinguish an object as the same subject of many manifestations, an ability that is involved with the subject-predicate structure of sentences, as we have seen in chapter two. No object is entirely the same when we perceive it anew; the new context always brings aspects that were not the same before, even though we may be assured of the object's continuity in all its contexts. But to cut through the similarities and continuities, to consider ourselves as perceiving once again the very same object, to consider the object as being the same for us as it was once before—all this involves a sense of identity which could not have been built up without language, and which ultimately could not have been reached except upon the basis of the strict identity and repetition which consonants provide. And until we are capable of so taking the object as identically the same, the object cannot present itself with this kind of identification, and this level of its ability to be truthful cannot be actualized. We are the conditions for the occurrence of its disclosure.

The possibility of repetition is strengthened even more in written language. Isak Dinesen describes, in *Out of Africa* (part II, chapter 3), something that we have long forgotten, the initial experience of writing, when its powers are most vivid because most distinguished from unwritten speech:

> The document now became Jogona's great treasure. . . . From time to time, mostly on Sunday mornings, he would suddenly appear in my door, lift the bag off and take out the paper to have it read to him. . . . At each reading his face took on the same impress of deep religious triumph, and after the reading he solicitously smoothed out his paper, folded it up and put it back in the bag. The importance of the account was not lessened but augmented with time, as if to Jogona the greatest wonder about it was that it did not change. The past, that had been so difficult to bring to memory, and that had probably seemed to be changing every time it was thought of, had here been caught, conquered and pinned down before his eyes.

The power of repetition, which is so strong in writing, is, however, only one of a whole series of identities and stabilities that the use of language permits; the establishment of phonemes is even more fundamental, even more forgotten, and even more difficult to describe in a story; and yet it has happened, with a shock that silences our babbling exuberance, to all of us.

Jakobson claims that a phoneme, whether consonant or vowel, is constituted by a bundle of sound features.[3] He says that in all languages studied so far, twelve distinctive factors operate; each factor is a binary opposition, like vocalic/non-vocalic, nasal/oral, abrupt/ continuant, and so on. Each phoneme is constituted by a choice made among several of these oppositions; for example /p/ and /b/ both choose the oral feature in the nasal/oral opposition, because neither involves any nasal resonance, but /p/ is voiceless and /b/ is voiced, so they differ in their choice within the opposition voiced/ voiceless. These phonemes would differ from still other phonemes by other choices made in other binary oppositions. Furthermore, the significant distinction among phonemes does not reside in any absolute sounds, but in how they are opposed to one another. When two speakers pronounce an /a/ in a given language, the sheer sound they make (the "phone") may be quite different; suppose, for example, one speaker is a Bostonian while the other is a Turk who speaks English as a foreign tongue. But this does not matter; the significant part is that each speaker can make clear a difference between his /a/ and, say, his /o/. It is the opposition among phonemes that makes them what they are.

Whether there are twelve binary oppositions for all languages, and which choices are made among them for a particular phoneme, are issues for linguists to discuss. What is interesting philosophically is the role of binary oppositions in the constitution of phonemes: the fact that each phoneme is the result of a selection of one alternative in each of several possible oppositions. Also interesting is the fact that a phoneme is not determined as an absolute sound, but as a sound opposed to other sounds—/p/ versus /b/, /a/ versus /o/—in a phonemic system. When a child leaves his babbling stage and enters into language, he becomes aware of the alternatives and begins to make these choices. He has to recast the sounds he has been making and now select them, and it is not surprising that sounds which were easy to make at random may be hard to recover as parts of a system of choices.

When he enters into language, even on the elementary level of phonemes, the speaker must sense binary oppositions and choose among them. It is, furthermore, not the case that he first possesses one of the alternatives, then the other, and finally the opposition between them; instead, the distinction between them comes "first" and establishes both members. Jakobson says that "in a child's mind the pair is anterior to isolated objects. The binary opposition is a child's first logical operation. Both opposites arise simultaneously and force the infant to choose one and to suppress the other of the two alternatives."[4] At the other extreme, when in aphasic illness linguistic abilities are lost, "a distinction ceases."[5] It is not that separate members are separately forgotten, like a cup and a saucer being individually lost, but the distinction between the opposites evaporates, and the opposites also cease to be.

There is something formally the same at work in the phonemic opposition, in the distinction inserted between an object and what the object is "taken as," in the distinction between a subject and its predicate, in the distinction established in naming between the object and its presence and absence. In all these the distinction is "prior" to the parts distinguished. The play of opposition, and the identity constituted within the opposition, come to full force in the use of language and in logic; however, they also range before and beyond language, as we shall see, through perception, memory, feeling, the continuity of objects, and the establishment of the mind and the self.

It is true that when adults speak a language, their attention is centered on whole words, sentences, and propositions; their explicit choices are made on these higher levels, and the selection of phonemes is not their direct concern. This is so because the choice of phonemes has become routine and is taken for granted, like the activity of walking, which is presupposed in playing football. But the phonemes are still the result of choices that once were made by someone, and they are still supported by the distinctions that establish them. And at the beginning of language in a child, the first selection of phonemes is equivalent to, and not presupposed by, the first establishment of words: "pa" and "ma" are among the first combined phonemes in a child's speech, and are used to name or call the most conspicuous objects the child has in its emerging world; first sounds, first objects. The phoneme /a/ is the first vowel because it is made by the open mouth with no articulation of sound, and /p/ is among the first consonants because it simply requires closing the mouth with the lips and interrupting the continuous vowel sound. Other phonemes are then built up by laws of development and implication that can be empirically determined. For example, the oral vowels become complicated by the addition of nasal resonance, then the shape of the mouth is altered to introduce more differences in sound. The consonantal clipping of vowels moves gradually from the front of the mouth to the back: lips, teeth, tongue come into play, and finally gutturals are produced in some languages. More complex phonemes presuppose the simpler ones—the German "ch," the Parisian "r," and the Bantu clicks could not be the first consonants executed by a child.

Phonemes are combined to form syllables, and then to form words; words combine to form sentences. A new kind of choice is available for the individual speaker on the level of sentences. He is able to select and combine words in ways he chooses, whereas his selection of phonemes and syllables is prescribed for him by the language he speaks. Although phonemes are the result of choices among various alternatives, the selection is made for us by the slow development of the language, and we must conform to what has been established, except in cases when we wish, for whatever effect, to do something that is patently idiosyncratic. This conformity imposed by the language ceases, in principle, once words are reached. We are given a much wider choice in the selection of words (house, hut, manse, dwelling, shack) and a range of possibilities in connecting them (the house was cold, the cold in the house, the house's being cold). There are rules that govern the substitution and the linkage of words, but they are not rigid, as phonemic regulations are. They offer many alternatives for the individual to choose from, and permit ingenuity and originality of style.

This offer of linguistic liberty is not accepted by everyone. Sentences and word phrases, and indeed whole arguments, are often repeated as wholes as routinely and as rigidly as words composed of phonemes and syllables.[6] But here the lack of originality is caused by an inability to take advantage of alternatives which are proposed, not by a lack of alternatives. And pressure for conformity comes not from the linguistic structure but from the general opinions and common expressions found in what everyone around us says.

As we have seen in chapter one, the syntax of a sentence must be more complete the more the speaker emerges into prominence and responsibility. The sentence must be a well-rounded whole if a particular report or registration is to be attributed to someone; if the linkage is deficient, the opinion in question cannot be adequately identified and we cannot be sure the man has said anything. But the originality and prominence of the speaker are also reflected in the lexicon, in his choice of names: if he responds to a phenomenon with standard names, what he says may as well have been said by anyone else; he is only slightly engaged in the activity of disclosure. A speaker, for example, hardly stands out by registering the fact that it is raining outside. But if he is able to make a deliberate choice of names to register and report more appropriately what is going on, he can make himself irreplaceable as a speaker and his voice will carry authority; no one else can express things the way he does.

Names and syntax provide two areas of choice in the formation of a sentence which are not available, for the individual speaker, in the selection and composition of phonemes into words. At this point we approach the problem of propositions and truth. We now ask what the speaker is trying to say, and we will no longer treat the sentence in function of its linguistic and phonemic parts, but in relation to this wider context.

Notes

1. David Diringer, *Writing* (London: Thames and Hudson, 1962), p. 49.

2. Roman Jakobson, *Child Language Aphasia and Phonological Universals* (The Hague: Mouton, 1972), pp. 21-22.

3. Roman Jakobson and Morris Halle, *Fundamentals of Language* (The Hague: Mouton, 1971), pp. 13-44.

4. *Fundamentals of Language*, pp. 60-61.

5. *Child Language Aphasia*, p. 32.

6. On the emergence of the speaker along with the achievement of judgments, see Robert Sokolowski, *Husserlian Meditations: How Words Present Things* (Evanston: Northwestern University Press, 1974), pp. 218-23.

CHAPTER 8

The Proposition as Achievement

How are propositions different from sentences? The proposition adds the dimension of truth to the sentence; there can be many sentences which do not intend to be involved with truth, like imperatives, exhortations, and emotive expressions, but a proposition is something put forward, proposed, as true.

Are propositions equivalent to declarative sentences then? Are they a species of sentence? No, and for four reasons. First, a declarative sentence or group of sentences is acceptably put together if it obeys the rules of grammatical correctness, but a proposition or group of propositions is acceptably put together only if, in addition to obeying the rules of correct grammar, it also conforms to the rules of consistency. Propositions cannot contradict themselves or each other and still remain seriously proposed as possibly true; but one sentence can "contradict" another sentence in a single discourse and both can still be uttered as correct sentences. They do not fail as sentences, as linguistic wholes. Secondly, the same proposition can be achieved in different sentences and in different languages. The sentence is a linguistic whole, and any changes in the language change the sentence, but they may leave the proposition intact. "The bridge was built in a week," "It took a week to build the bridge," "Innerhalb einer Woche wurde die Brücke gebaut," are different sentences expressing the same proposition, which could be repeated in an indefinite number of translations. Thirdly, the context of utterance can cause a change in what is proposed as true, even though the sentence remains the same: "The Prime Minister of England is a tall man" is a sentence that can be used to make different propositions, depending on whether it is stated when this man or that is in office. This third reason, which has been used by Strawson to show that propositions are not reducible to sentences, is the antithesis of the second, in which different sentences express the same proposition.[1]

The fourth reason we have for distinguishing between sentence and proposition is provided by Husserl: it is possible for us to achieve a perfect sentence, one which obeys the rules of grammar and selects the appropriate names of things, while we as yet judge or propose only vaguely.[2] Vagueness and indistinctness are terms introduced by Husserl to name a phenomenon of utmost philosophical importance. Simply stated, vagueness means that although we may speak correctly, we do not understand what we are saying. The proposal we are making as true is obscure. In contrast, distinct judging is the case when, in addition to uttering a proper sentence, we also "make a thought." We think while we speak, we achieve the proposition, we articulate its syntactical parts and explicitly choose its lexical elements. The difference between distinct and indistinct judging is not the same as the difference which Ryle, for example, has examined, between parroting, or the mechanical, rote repetition of words on one hand, and serious speech on the other; that is an easy and relatively unimportant distinction, because no one takes parroting as real speech.[3] We are concerned with what seems to be thoughtful speech but really is not; to discriminate between this and truly thoughtful speech is to raise the difference between sophistry and knowledge, appearances and what is real, the associative and the logical. This is the hunting ground for philosophy. Even logic does not understand its own subject matter if the difference between distinct and indistinct judging is not made clear, because logic examines the structures which work specifically in the distinct proposition.

In order to avoid psychologism, some philosophers like Frege claimed that propositions or senses belonged to a realm of being distinct from psychological acts and ordinary material objects. Strawson, by involving the context of utterance in the determination of propositional meaning, moves counter to this tendency to detach propositions from speakers; he takes into account the proposition's attachment to a speaker and to a situation. However, even acknowledging the context of utterance does not yet introduce the dimension we discuss now, the fact that the sentence can be perfectly achieved while the propositional achievement, the categorial performance, is only indistinct; that is, while the thinking is obscure. It seems to have been taken for granted that thoughtless speech is of only marginal interest philosophically, that philosophy can begin its inquiry with thoughtful speaking as the standard case, accepted as simply there with no need of clarification. Perhaps this was done because scientific discourse, in which a technical competence in using the language is assumed, has been implicitly used as the paradigm for speech; and when science is not used, then rather simple registrations and reports are often employed as models, like saying that the grass is green or the cat is on the rug, statements that are easy to achieve distinctly in normal circumstances. But instead of taking distinctness for granted, the emergence of thoughtful out of thoughtless speech, the transition from vague, obscure, indistinct judging to distinct articulation, is a subject we must explore philosophically if we are to understand what a proposition is and what thinking and truth are. A proposition is not to be contrasted to sheer silence or mute sensibility, and thinking is not to be contrasted to a totally blank mind; these are not the appropriate "contraries" to be used in our definitions. Using them would be like trying to define man by contrasting him not with animals but with vegetables. Instead, the proposition is to be contrasted to the propositionless sentence, and thinking is to be constrasted to thoughtless speech. Attention to this issue places the philosophy of language in a central position in political philosophy. It makes us aware of the emergence of a responsible and authoritative speaker, who is distinguished, by what he says, from those who use language indistinctly and without responsibility. We come to appreciate the difference between one who knows and those who chatter. We become concerned with the owner of a given speech and the proposer of a certain judgment; and his intellectual character, whether worthy of admiration or of disregard, becomes a philosophical theme. None of these dimensions come forward until the problem of obscurity versus distinctness in speech and judgment is faced.

Neither propositions nor speakers leap out of silence; they arise from the vague use of language.

We have mentioned four reasons for distinguishing between sentence and proposition: the dimension of consistency as a factor beyond sentential correctness; the possibility of one proposition in many sentences through translation and paraphrase; the possibility of several propositions in the use of a single sentence because of a change in the speaker and the context of utterance; the possibility of a vaguely achieved proposition in a distinctly executed sentence. All these reasons are, in effect, indications of a dimension which is different from the sentential, although necessarily involved with it. The first reason mentions a property of propositions that distinguishes them from sentences; the second and third claim that either the proposition or the sentence can change while the other remains the same; the fourth claims the proposition may be unsatisfactorily achieved while the sentence is adequately completed.

The proposition is a composed whole. It involves some elements which serve to connect others; these are the syntactical parts. It also involves the elements that are joined by the syntax; let us call these the cores or core parts of the proposition. Later we will see how the cores and syntax of the proposition are related to the names and grammar of the sentence.

Following Husserl, let us distinguish three aspects in the way a proposition can be composed.[4] First, there is the question whether the proposition is *syntactically well formed:* if it fails in this respect, it is not a proposition at all, but only a heap of terms. For example, a "proposal" made up of a proper name, a conjunction, an alternation, and an implication, in that order, is not a proposition. It fails in its syntax, it is not properly put together, it does not constitute a whole sense. Secondly, supposing that a proposition or a series of propositions is well formed, we can ask whether it is *consistent* or not: does it contradict itself? Does it make a certain move in its syntax, and then make another move that annuls the first? Propositions can be well formed or meaningful and yet inconsistent, and the issue of consistency concerns the linkage, the syntax: are the propositions so put together that they destroy one another or themselves? Thirdly, is the proposition or the series of propositions *coherent*: here not the syntax but the cores arranged by the syntax are the issue. Do the cores blend properly? A proposition like "The man died of his illness and the doctors then helped him get well again" is well formed syntactically and is also formally consistent, but it is incoherent, since "getting well after dying" is not a possible combination of propositional cores. Being well formed, being consistent, and being coherent are three aspects of the proposition which must be distinctly treated, although obviously they are never found apart from one another.

We have already distinguished between the vague and the distinct execution of the proposition. Propositions are achieved by someone at some place and at some time; in their concrete existence they can be vaguely or distinctly achieved. Vagueness can harbor both inconsistency and incoherence. When the proposition is brought to distinctness, its inconsistency and incoherence, if it has any, become manifest, and of course we reappraise our assertion of it. We may even find, on reaching distinctness, that what we possessed vaguely was not even well formed in its propositional syntax, but the cases of inconsistency and incoherence are more common.

Vagueness exists when we passively accept a position which we cursorily read, or which we hear, or which just happens to come to mind. These are the examples which Husserl gives. We hold the opinion and may even, indistinctly, repeat it, but we have not thought it through; we do possess it vaguely, however, and are able subsequently to bring it to distinctness. We then "appropriate" it, make it on our own, make it our own. But Husserl makes his task easier by limiting himself to such examples; they are all cases where we are easily able to move from vagueness to distinctness once we put our minds to it. This claim, that everyone can bring to distinctness any vague judgment which he makes, is a symptom of Husserl's rationalism. Far more interesting and important philosophically are the propositions that achieve a vague existence but are doomed to remain forever in an obscure condition, at least in some minds. It is not just a matter of something we passively hear and have not yet gotten around to achieving explicitly; there are judgments whose vagueness in certain minds will never be dispersed, not because the person in question is remiss in applying his attention to the issue, but because he does not know a move toward distinctness needs to be made, and could not make it even if he suspected something of the sort was necessary. It is not a question of good or bad will, and while we might admire someone's ability to judge distinctly, we cannot really blame someone else who does not have it. It is not the result of choice. This obscurity pervading what we actually say about things is the ignorance that Plato's Socrates found in most men—it was not a failure to know certain facts or formulas—and his merit lay solely in being aware of this condition, of knowing the difference between vagueness and its corresponding distinctness. By supplementing Husserl's rather harmless instances of vagueness with this ineradicable kind, with all the political, humane, and ethical issues it involves, we can implicate his thoughts on logic with themes in political philosophy and with the problem of the responsible speaker, as distinguished from the mouthpiece of what others say.

The nature of vagueness may be further clarified by an example intermediate between the two extremes we have mentioned, between cases in which we must only pay attention to scatter the obscurity and cases in which the vagueness can never be dispelled. Sometimes we may be unable to execute the propositions distinctly at the present time, but with training we might become capable of doing so. This can be exemplified in the way a book is read by a student beginning work in a particular field and the way it is read by someone who is able to write a book just like it. The beginner cannot authentically achieve the propositions expressed in the book, but he may be able to do so later.

Practically every judgment we make distinctly is first with us vaguely. Even if we are being told something by others—unless we are just about ready to have the same thought ourselves—we first get a loose grip on the statement by achieving the sentence, and then we think it through. When we do so, we may find that what we earlier entertained is indeed coherent and consistent, or we may find that it is not: its cores may not blend properly, or it may resolve itself into two propositions which annul one another. What was uttered or written as one is really composed of two locked in combat, like Esau and Jacob in the womb of Rebecca. This struggle is not manifest until distinctness is achieved; it may never become known to the one in whose mind it exists, and yet it can be made clear to someone else who thinks about what that person is saying.

The transition from vagueness to distinctness affords yet another set of differences in which the proposition can be identified. Besides being able to have the same proposition in many translations or in many repetitions, we now have it as vague and as distinct. What we achieve distinctly is recognized as the same judgment we earlier executed vaguely; even if it shatters into two irreconcilable statements, the two are the same as what was previously taken as one.

The person emerges as a speaker concomitantly with the positions he takes; his mind becomes actualized only when he achieves propositions distinctly. He is there as a human being before that; he is there as a physical organism, as someone with a history of perceptions, memories, and a way of doing things, as a speaker of a certain language, as the repetitor of opinions that he inhales from the air about him; but until he has used his mother tongue to achieve distinct propositions, there is a dimension in his being that has not become actual. Knowing a language is not yet being able to think in the language. He may even achieve moral virtues, such as courage, temperance, and generosity, and so become a praiseworthy man; but moral virtues are not the same as intellectual ones, and he may still not have made many judgments that are conspicuously his own.

Furthermore, even many of the remarks we make about things we perceive may not be distinct judgments. My casual reports or registrations that it is sunny outside, that it has been a sleepy day, that the door is open, are not taken over from what others say, but they are not conspicuous enough to be my own opinions. Such remarks, although they have a sentential form, operate more like the gerundial reactions we have contrasted to sentences in chapter two. They are rather mechanical linguistic reactions, not deliberately chosen names and syntax; anyone in my position who spoke my language would say the same thing; no one would normally attribute it to me specifically as my position. There may be extraordinary circumstances when even such trivial items may be important and require a distinct proposition, or may require serious scrutiny and an authoritative remark; but normally they do not: an automatic response suffices. On the other hand, there are propositions, like those made by Samuel Johnson, which are thoroughly the property of some one person and are distinguished by being his opinions. No one else could have formulated them, and few would have noticed the fact that they record; when others repeat them they know they are conforming their minds to the actuality and achievement of another's. Psychologically there are two minds at work, but the actuality of mind shared by both belongs to Samuel Johnson; it comes to life again in the man who repeats what he said. There is one thought, one proposition in both minds. This repetition of opinions in other minds is what makes possible the rule of certain minds over others, a rule which is considered by Machiavelli as the most complete and easy dominion, once it has been achieved (*The Prince,* chapter 11; *Discourses,* chapter 11).

Acquiring an identity as a speaker, as someone who has distinguished opinions, is especially related to the formal consistency of the propositions one makes; formal logic is directly concerned with the consistency of a particular series of propositions, but it presupposes the fact that the body of statements it examines is presented as assertible by a single speaker. Only when this is understood do formal conflicts in what is said become important. Of course every proposition that is made by anyone is made as assertible by all, since it is put forward as true, so logic in its actual practice can afford to overlook the unity of the speaker behind the speech and pay attention simply to the arrangement of propositions. But since propositions do not arrange themselves, and need to be achieved and held together by somebody, the voice that holds them cannot be neglected in a philosophical account of what logic does. Furthermore, the identity of a speaker does not continue only through a particular speech, long as it might be. It makes him the owner of everything he says throughout his lifetime, and he cannot without justification annul statements he has once made, if his speech is to be responsible.

A step in the syntax or linkage of a proposition has to be achieved; like the proposition as a whole, each syntactical step is a product which requires an activity by a speaker each time it is actualized. When we speak inconsistently, we apparently achieve a certain proposition and then later do something that annuls the achievement. We might do this by performing the same proposition again, but with an element that dissolves what we earlier put together; or we may carry out a new proposition which by its formal implications annuls the one done earlier. We do something and then we undo it, we produce something and then we dismantle it. It is not a question of two things that eliminate one another, like two hostile animals, but of two achievements that cancel one another, and of a single achiever who tries to do both: for such speakers, as Plato says, "the foe is in their own household, as the saying goes, and, like that queer fellow Eurycles, they carry about with them wherever they go a voice in their own bellies to contradict them" (*Sophist* 252C). The fact that both positions are held together in and accomplished by one speaker is what makes them of serious logical interest. Someone who tries to affirm as one what is really an incompatible pair clearly does so because his achievement falls short of what it should be; if someone shows him this inconsistency by bringing it to distinctness, Plato observes, "He, seeing this, is angry with himself and grows gentle toward others" (*Sophist* 230B).

Conflicts in vagueness can result from either the syntax or the cores of the propositions. The syntax may require complex moves of composition which the speaker cannot execute and which he cannot hold together as a whole; it is analogous to a complicated and deft maneuver in basketball—a move to the right, a turn, a feint, a pass—which some players cannot carry out without falling over. Instead of really doing the steps, a player may make a few feeble, "vague" gestures this way and that and think he has carried out the play. And instead of doing the intellectual moves, the speaker lets himself be carried along by words he associates with the subject at hand and with linkage that seems to him to be apt, and he winds up saying things that deny what he said before. More commonly, however, the vagueness stems from what is named in the cores of the propositions. The cores may be nominalized facts that are very complex and their implications subtle; the speaker uses names to cover them, but he never did and could not now unravel the cores, so he does not know what they imply. Instead of following out implications, his mind is pulled by associations and he is led to say things that contradict his earlier statements. Besides the complexities enfolded in the cores, what is named in them might simply be things he has not become acquainted with, and so he repeats what he has generally heard about this issue rather than what he has learned himself to be true about it. By letting others speak through him, he runs the risk of not speaking as a single, consistent voice. Thus the obscurity pervading the cores of his propositions can lead to inconsistency in their syntax. It can also lead to incoherence, but that failure must be distinguished from contradiction, from annulment of what was said before. Along still another line, statements can become inconsistent when the speaker is emotionally aroused or speaking compulsively, but then his speech becomes less a proposal of true statements and more a symptom of feeling; what he says ceases even to claim consistency.

The vague use of language, which provides us with the opportunity of becoming distinct in our thought, when not used toward this end makes us adopt the ridiculous posture of an inconsistent speaker. We are immersed not only in language but in the unowned opinions that "everybody" knows, which give our language a configuration; we do not pick up bits and pieces of grammar and names at first, but opinions which are made up of grammar and names. These opinions are not attributable to any particular speaker; they are what "they" say. No one is responsible for them, so it is not surprising that they contradict one another. They pull and push one another by association, coming together and repelling each other because of contiguity, resemblance, and constant conjunction. Someone who inhales these opinions along with his language and simply breathes them out again, perhaps in a new order, will be as inconsistent as "they" are. Idea-clots coalesce in him, and floating opinions come together in what he says, but until he moves toward distinctness, he has no identifiable voice, and logic is a vague threat rather than a serious problem. What he says, including the sequence and composition of his sentences, is coincidental.

The problem of consistency is rarely an issue in trivial remarks about things, but it becomes conspicuous in what people have to say about such subjects as politics, human affairs, religion, literature, justification for what people have done, economics, law, and the like. It is especially important in what are generally called "philosophical" remarks about things.[5] Often discussions of such topics are a raging flood of vagueness, and someone who sees it as vagueness may be almost reduced to silence, hardly able to decide what issue ought to be salvaged, brought to distinctness, in this universal wreck. The inconsistency that hides in vagueness, where contradictions are unwittingly entertained, must of course be distinguished from paradoxes, in which the speaker deliberately chooses contradictory propositions, either for rhetorical effect or because the matter cannot be better grasped at the time. The speaker of paradoxes knows what he is doing; the speaker caught in vagueness does not. Finally, the inconsistencies in vagueness are obviously not lies. When a liar deliberately says things he knows are untrue, he will sooner or later be forced into contradictions with other statements he must make about other aspects of the true fact. Therefore detective stories almost always resolve themselves into a clever disclosure of inconsistency in what the guilty party says or between what he says and what he does, letting him condemn himself out of his own mouth. A lie is a chosen and purposely concealed inconsistency; vagueness is innocent of its contradictions, regrettable but not deserving of blame.

The self as speaker or as mind contains a part which is not truly himself when he entertains judgments vaguely; the mind of the self in vagueness is misty. We are always partly vague, but is it not legitimate to say that to this extent we are always partly not ourselves? Someone else, or an anonymous voice, is speaking through us; our minds are not self-formed. Have we not all felt that when we get caught having said something that turns out to be vague and inconsistent, the tendency is to dissociate ourselves from this position, to apologize that it really was not us talking? And there is in every vague position a glimpse of something we expect to become distinct—provided we can differentiate between the obscure and the distinct—and this is what we incipiently appropriate even while it is still vague. Vagueness, with all its anonymity and carelessness, has the embryo of distinctness and responsibility in it; it contains the distinctable, though not yet the distinct. Furthermore, we must distinguish between people who have been both vague and distinct and who know the difference between the two, and others who have for all practical purposes only been vague; the former may be culpable if they choose to remain in obscurity on an important issue, but the latter are beyond responsibility.

A remark of Samuel Johnson in his *Journey to the Western Islands of Scotland* illustrates the distinction between achieving a sentence, which can be done with strength, clarity, and vividness, and achieving a distinct proposition, which, in contrast to the sentence, may fail completely:

> He that travels in the Highlands may easily saturate his soul with intelligence, if he will acquiesce in the first account. The Highlander gives to every question an answer so prompt and peremptory, that skepticism itself is dared into silence, and the mind sinks before the bold reporter in unresisting credulity; but, if a second question be ventured, it breaks the enchantment; for it is immediately discovered, that what was told so confidently was told at hazard, and that such fearlessness of assertion was either the sport of negligence, or the refuge of ignorance.[6]

The passage recognizes that behind the confident sentence there was no proposition, but only the hazard of association, which brings along the inevitable contradiction; and Johnson also knows that contradictory assertions bespeak an inconsistent mind, for his next sentence begins with the phrase, "If individuals are thus at variance with themselves. . . ." The effect such discourse has on one who hears it is also described: "Such is the laxity of Highland conversation, that the inquirer is kept in continual suspense, and by a kind of intellectual retrogradation, knows less as he hears more."

It can be misleading to say that in vagueness the speaker first makes one proposition or propositional move and later makes another that annuls the first. This would imply that a distinct proposal is achieved and then destroyed. In fact, no explicit judgment is made, and the inconsistency is merely a sign that the speaker did not take a specific position in the first place, although his words suggested that he did. The inconsistency is recognized only by someone who does achieve a distinct judgment on the basis of what is spoken, like Johnson in his conversations with the Highlanders.

When he hears his "first account" he executes it as a judgment, and he is later distressed to hear a statement unsaying the first; but no distinct proposition was ever achieved by the speaker. Johnson himself later explains the Highlanders' tendency to self-contradiction by their incapacity to bring about a judgment which is, decisively, either true or false: "They have inquired and considered little, and do not always feel their own ignorance. They are not much accustomed to be interrogated by others; and seem never to have thought of interrogating themselves; so that if they do not know what they tell to be true, they likewise do not distinctly perceive it to be false." The consequence of this is immediately mentioned: "Mr. Boswell was very diligent in his inquiries; and the result of his investigations was, that the answer to the second question was commonly such as nullified the answer to the first."[7]

Notes

1. For example, see "Propositions, Concepts, and Logical Truth," in *Logico-Linguistic Papers* (London: Methuen, 1971), pp. 117, 124-25; in the same volume, "Singular Terms and Predication," pp. 59-64, and "Identifying Reference and Truth Values," pp. 80-81.

2. Edmund Husserl, *Formal and Transcendental Logic*, trans. D. Cairns (The Hague: Nijhoff, 1969), §16 and Appendix II; see Robert Sokolowski, *Husserlian Meditations: How Words Present Things* (Evanston: Northwestern University Press, 1974), §73-§81.

3. See Gilbert Ryle, *Collected Papers* (London: Hutcheson, 1971), vol. 2, pp. 15, 231-32, 291, 454, 468, 488. Ryle's description of the experience of perplexity or difficulty in thinking (v.g., p. 259) does not get at the phenomenon we are concerned with either; in what we are describing, the person does not know he is thinking indistinctly.

4. *Formal and Transcendental Logic*, §14, §15, §89, and Appendix I. Earlier versions of these distinctions occur in *Logical Investigations*.

5. See Robert Sokolowski, *Husserlian Meditations: How Words Present Things*, §81, §86-§89.

6. Samuel Johnson, *A Journey to the Western Islands of Scotland*, ed. R. W. Chapman (New York: Oxford University Press, 1970), p. 45.

7. *Ibid.*, pp. 106-107.

CHAPTER 9

The Proposition as a Rule for Sentences

The proposition, what we propose as true, has parts; the sentence also has parts. Are the parts of the proposition exactly isomorphic with those of the sentence? Is every grammatical and lexical unit mapped onto the proposition? If this were so, it would be hard to see why sentence and proposition should be at all distinguished.

There are two extremes to be avoided in this issue. The first is what we have just mentioned, that the proposition be a carbon copy of the sentence. The difficulty with this is that no translation or paraphrase would be possible, because what we assert would be precisely this sentence, with its peculiar twists of grammar and choice of names; but we do find that translations and variations in sentences, sometimes slight and sometimes extensive, allow us still to make the same point. Furthermore, the propositional dimensions we have discussed in the last chapter, consistency and distinctness, do not seem to be accounted for in this position.

The other extreme is to carry out radical surgery on the sentence, to reduce all its grammatical moves to a very few irreducible ones, like conjunction, predication, negation, and quantification, and to dismiss whatever is left as not part of the proposition. In effect, this position wishes to melt down all moves of linkage to those which are required to state the truth conditions of the assertion. As we have seen, the conjunction "but" can be reduced, as far as the issue of truth and verification goes, to the simple conjunction "and." "But" is used in a rhetorical way, with the response of the listener in mind; the phrase that precedes it arouses an expectation in him, and the "but" counteracts this expectation: "He came, but he did not stay." As far as the truth of this proposition is concerned, "and" would do quite as well; the statement is true simply if both phrases are true, whether we use "and" or "but." Now the extreme position we are examining would claim that every grammatical move which is not one of the few elementary moves we accept as indispensable for truth can be dismissed as a rhetorical device used in consideration of the listener and his responses; it has no effect on the truth of what is being proposed, it looks to the interlocutor and not to the objects discussed. Even more superfluous, it may be there only as an ornament. For example, a sentence that has the form: S_1 is Pa, and S_2, which is Pb, is Pd although S_3 is Pc; could be equated with: S_1 is Pa, S_2 is Pd, S_2 is Pb, S_3 is Pc, four simple predications. The subordinations and concessions are all for the benefit of the interlocutor and do not form part of the proposition as a structure involving what is true. And because subordinations do not count, nominalization of a fact or proposition does not matter either, because nominalizing is a procedure to achieve subordination. All nominalized propositions are unpacked and spread out in an undifferentiated chain of simple, "atomic" propositions.

This is clearly excessive. Some clauses in a proposition are obviously intended as subordinate, nominalized clauses, which are not asserted as prominently as the main predication in the proposition; the main assertion is asserted because the subordinate clauses are taken for granted. Also, even though many grammatical elements in a sentence look to the response of the interlocutor, they still belong in the proposition: the sense of "but" is meant for anyone who wants to repeat the statement; the particular points are arranged in this way, with this sense of contrast, and a speaker might well feel his meaning is distorted if the contrast is left out. This radical surgery removes too much. But then how are we to avoid falling back into the other extreme, in which every grammatical nuance becomes a significant part of the proposition, the sentence and the proposition collapse into one, and translation and paraphrase become impossible?

To resolve this dilemma we must turn to the speaker and his intentions. The only one who can decide whether or not a certain grammatical move is essential to what is being said is the one who knows what the speaker is trying to say. Any language gives alternative formulations for almost any construction: "within a week," "before a week was over," "by week's end," "it takes a week"; "he was weary," "weariness came upon him," "he was filled with weariness." The grammatical moves in each of these groups differ from one another, yet in very many cases we can imagine a speaker thinking that what he wants to assert is perfectly conveyed by any one of them. The grammatical variations and complexities all cover and express a single propositional move. What is the move? Can we display it in its simplicity, by itself, stripped of its many possible alternative expressions in grammar? We cannot: we can only give one of its grammatical, sentential expressions, with an awareness that alternatives are available. Propositions and their parts are accessible only in sentences and their parts, and in no other way; this is why it is so difficult to distinguish between the two. In this respect, propositions are no different from any other object presented to us; everything we know is an identity that can appear in a manifold of appearances. The cube is what can be seen from this side and from that, the tragedy is what can be performed by the Old Vic and by the dramatics club, the sentence is what can be said by me or by him, in a high or low voice. To say that a proposition or one of its parts must be identified with this sentence or this grammatical expression is like saying the cube is only what can be seen from this side.

Of course there may be times when a speaker deliberately chooses between "within a week" and "before a week was over." He may wish to assert this and not that. He has not chosen randomly or for euphony or ornament among the alternatives the language gives him, but because he wants to say one and not the other. Then what he chooses becomes part of the proposition. But only he or someone thinking distinctly along with him can make this discrimination.

Does not everyone deliberately choose every grammatical move and sentential part? No; even someone who thinks carefully while he speaks or writes lets himself be carried by some automatic consolidations in his language and its grammar. Only rarely does deliberate choice extend to every last element in each sentence; this is scarce enough in writing, and almost impossible in speech. We have to let some choices be gross if we are to keep the speech alive. People who try to select every detail of their sentences when they talk, to carry out every comma, strangle themselves in their speech; this is a professional danger of persons learned in languages. They know the most minute options their language provides and cannot forbear explicit choices, even when discussing quite ordinary matters, on this level. Their sentences become ends in themselves, not vehicles used for public thinking, not subservient to what is supposed to be said. Such persons are comic figures precisely because they achieve only sentences, clouds of sentences, in which the proposition cannot be found, and in which the linguistic grammar gets in the way of propositional syntax. But even more thoughtless, more devoid of proposition, is the other extreme, in which the speaker chooses hardly at all but just repeats linguistic, grammatical wholes taken in enormous portions from what everybody says about the issue at hand.

There is no way to avoid mentioning the intelligent speaker and his intentions in making the distinction between merely sentential parts and effective propositional parts. There are no criteria that can be applied automatically to the sentence to discriminate; we cannot say all adverbs, or all commas, or all concessive conjunctions, or all passive verb forms are merely sentential and not propositional. Anything can be included as part of the proposition if the speaker intends it to be included; and yet given the passive, vague use of language that has to underlie even the most intelligent speech, there must be some sentential parts that do not count as propositional. Of course, not only the speaker, but an intelligent listener too discriminates between the merely sentential and the propositional. This is inevitable, since the speech is also executed, in that peculiar pursuant way, by those who hear the speaker's voice and understand what he means. Sometimes the listener may be more intelligent than the speaker, and may see that some sentential parts are really superfluous, even though the speaker thinks he is making essential moves. We experience this vividly at times when someone else gives us our thoughts back in a more direct, incisive way than we had believed possible; he cuts the proposition loose from the sentence we merged it with.

If we deal with writing, where the "speaker" of the sentences is no longer available for questioning, the same discrimination between the merely sentential and the propositional must still be made, but now by an intelligent reader. However, although there is one author for a given text, there cannot be any one definitive reader; others will always come along. Hence the importance of establishing an accurate text and keeping it intact, to make available to others the exact sentences in which the play of the linguistic and the propositional must occur; hence also the subordinate role of those who labor to establish the text, because unless the sentential is distinguished from the propositional by somebody—unless the text is thought through—it possesses only antiquarian value.

Spoken and written sentences are differentiated from their propositions by a pair of interlocutors, either speaker and listener or author and reader. There is one text and two minds. The reverse occurs in the case of translation: here two texts, two sentences, are mediated by a single mind, and they are said to express one proposition. All translation resolves itself into an activity performed by one individual who knows both languages. Something is said in one language, and he says it in the other. Only he can determine if the translation is satisfactory, if the same thing is being said. It may well be impossible to say exactly the same thing if the languages are very different, like English and Swahili, but our intelligent mediator at least knows that one translation is closer than another. This improvement, this possibility of recognizing better and worse, shows that there is more sameness in some cases than in others. The judge of whether or not two sentences express the same proposition is the thoughtful speaker of both languages, not any automatic set of correspondences that can be established by theories concerning the languages or by a manual of translation. And while the speaker of one language is learning the rudiments of a new tongue, he is not yet translating nor is he thinking in the new language. He is making practice gestures that will enable him later to think and translate. His use of language is not even a kind of judging in vagueness; he must acquire linguistic competence for that to happen. His practice remarks are analogous to sentences found as examples in grammar books, disconnected from any assertion and from any proposal. True, he already speaks one language, so he cannot approach the new one as a child; he has become accustomed to naming and can never make that transition again. But the grammatical moves he executes are not propositional positions which he takes, they are attempts to prepare for them.

Translation between languages and understanding between different cultural forms are rendered possible on an advanced level by persons who speak both languages and by persons who have lived in both cultures. Even when we begin without the benefit of such double formation, however, when people from totally different cultures meet for the very first time, there are vast areas of common ground in human experience which provide a starting point for translation and mutual understanding and set us on the chain of better and worse translations, closer and farther interpretations. All men get hungry and thirsty, are warm and chilly, and see the possibility of talking to one another. In these and innumerable other respects there are forms of "taking as" that we all share, and the student of a new language tries, in his practice moves, to integrate the new linguistic forms with his ways of taking things. Someone who discovers a new group of people does not begin his dealings with them by proposing and soliciting the registration of facts and the names of things; he first must get involved in doing things and reacting to them in the company of his new interlocutors. If an anthropologist or a linguist, like the one imagined by Quine in *Word and Object* (chapter 7), wants to ask some remote tribe about their names for what he calls rabbits, he first has to arrive there, get a place to stay, share some food, greet the natives, and so on. He does not materialize as an interrogator out of thin air; having a voice with which to make sentences implies having a body, and the basic needs of the body follow similar lines for everyone. Although science may claim to think from no restricted viewpoint and from no special place or time, the scientist has to speak and write his sentences, and as a condition for this he has to eat, drink, and rest, and language is used in a nontheoretical way in getting these things done. Furthermore, besides getting settled, the investigator has to get the idea across to the natives that he is talking to them and not roaring or burping. More problematic still, he must make them understand he is asking them questions, inviting assent and dissent, and he must understand how assent and dissent are expressed, before he can get involved with particular names and observation sentences. Language is born in our active involvement with others, and it becomes theoretical or observational, as Heidegger has shown, only through an adjustment of its practical use.

If sentences have to be used by an intelligent speaker in order that a proposition be achieved, perhaps there is no need to claim the proposition is an identity of its own. Could it be reduced to the thoughtful behavior of the speaker? Could the proposition be simply the activity of proposing? The activity of the speaker is necessary, just as it is for achieving a sentence, word, or phoneme, but "the proposal" is an achievement beyond the activity. It is not, of course, a material object, nor is it something that could be achieved separately from the sentence—any more than the sentence could be produced apart from the achievement of words and phonemes. But it can be made thematic and identified as the same over and over again; we can make it again when we repeat it, we can come back to it, use it as a premise, use it as a subject of predication in a more complex proposition. Even the possibility of denying a proposition means that it is there again to be denied. It is available as an identity in the many peculiar manifolds of appearance which present it. Also, if we are thoughtful and so recognize the proposition, we can know when it is available and when it is not: we recognize when someone has achieved it (in distinctness) and when he is aiming at it but not producing it (in vagueness). The identity of a proposition is not that much different from the kind of identity, the kind of being, enjoyed by the sente ̀e, which hardly anyone would deny as "being the same" each time it is uttered.

But what kind of identity does the proposition enjoy? It is clearly not a material thing, and Husserl, in agreement with many other philosophers, has called it an "ideal" being.[1] He tries to clarify this by comparing it to other cases of ideal entities, such as a drama or a symphony or some other "cultural object." He says no one would deny that Beethoven's Seventh Symphony is somehow identically the same "object" whenever it is played, or that *Hamlet* is individually a single play even though the acts of performing it are different each time. Similarly, Husserl claims, the proposition or judgment is the same even though the judgings are different and only similar to one another.

Husserl's claim secures the identity of the proposition by including it in a wider class of ideal objects, and makes us less uncomfortable in agreeing that a proposition has some sort of existence distinguishable from the sentence. But he does not explain or even sufficiently describe the identity of the proposition; he simply classifies it. And there are important differences between propositions and symphonies that are not brought out when they are so cursorily compared. Can we be more specific about the identity of the proposition?

The proposition can be taken as a special kind of rule. It is different from most rules in the following respect. Most rules are formulated or expressed in an action which is different from the behavior that they govern. For example, a golf swing is a rule-governed action; it should conform to certain directions for holding the club and moving the body. The directions, the rules, are formulated in words. To state the rules is not to swing the club, but to achieve something that governs the swinging of the club. The expression of the rule and the performance of the action in accordance with the rule are two different activities: to say "You should keep your left arm straight when you swing the club back" is different from keeping the left arm straight when I swing back. Likewise the rules for changing a tire on a car are expressed in a linguistic activity which is different from actually changing the tire: to say "One should first jack the car up till the tire barely touches the ground, then remove the hub cap and wheel bolts" is different from doing these things.

The use of language, like any activity, is also governed by rules which are expressible apart from the activities they govern. There are rules concerning the position of the lips and tongue, the engagement of the larynx, and the like for achieving each phoneme, and they are formulated apart from achieving the phoneme. There are rules for syllable and word construction. There are also grammatical rules that govern the composition of a sentence, and they too are expressed quite apart from the grammatical moves they govern: I need not use a perfect participle to say how the perfect participle should be used.

Any sentence is therefore governed by many rules concerning its phonemes, words, and grammar, and these rules are expressed in sentences different from the sentence they govern. But in addition, if the sentence is thoughtful, it is also governed by a rule of composition which is expressed by the sentence itself. This rule is the sentence's proposition. This rule does not engender the phonemes, words, and grammar—it supposes that they have been produced according to their proper rules—but it controls how all these things come together in the sentence. In other words, we have not done enough with a sentence if we have given a phonemic, philological, etymological, and grammatical analysis of it; it still reflects the pressure and force of another governing principle, the thought, which also finds expression in it. If we grasp the thought, we can understand why the speaker or writer chose these words, these grammatical moves, this order and emphasis, and even perhaps certain violations of grammatical rules and certain oddities of lexical usage, such as metaphors, in his sentence. If the grasp of this rule is left out, we are to the sentence like investigators of an organism who know everything about it except that it is alive.

The peculiarity of the proposition as a rule is that it is also expressed in the sentence it governs. It cannot be made available in any other way. At best, we can provide a paraphrase, but then we simply have another sentence governed by the same propositional rule. We cannot formulate it separately as a rule, we can only give instances of its sentential governance. If we go into another language, we get still another sentence governed by and expressing it; we may find the obedience of this language to the rule highly unsatisfactory, and perhaps some propositions simply could not find the materials to organize a sentence in the present condition of the language; but there are always some areas of common ground, and the very attempt to obey the propositional rule sets us on the continuum of approximations, of better and worse cases, of expressing it. The language itself, its grammatical and lexical possibilities, starts to feel the pressure of the rule intruding on its sentences and will accommodate itself to it as time goes on.

The fact that a proposition can only be expressed in one of its governed sentences makes it different from other cultural objects, such as musical compositions; they too govern their expressions, but can be formulated in a score apart from them. In this they are like ordinary rules. Even a drama, insofar as it involves acting as well as words, has stage rules that are different from the performances they govern. It is in this respect that a proposition differs from other cultural objects.

Taking a proposition as this special sort of rule may make us less reluctant to admit the identity of a proposition in many sentential utterances. There is less danger of imagining the proposition or the thought as a crystalline thing somehow behind the sentence and separable from it. To say the same rule effectively governs many different sentential compositions is less perplexing; it is plausible enough to say there is one and the same rule controlling many sentences, spoken by many speakers, and even in many languages. But of course the rule does more than just govern the sentence; it is expressed by it and is thereby actually given in the sentence, which is one member of the manifold of its proper appearances. The rule does not govern the sentence at a distance—at a linguistic and temporal distance, as it would if it, like other rules, were capable of being formulated apart from what it governs—but in immediate contact with it. The rule *is* there.

The different possibilities of language allow some interesting variations on this. If we read publicly a speech we have written earlier, it is possible that we thought while we·wrote it but that our reading is less thoughtful and more concerned with the mechanics of delivery; and yet the propositions governing and expressed by the sentences are there for the listeners who think along with the reading. Writing allows this sort of delayed presence. But the most elementary case of propositional presence is a speech extempore. If a serious issue arises and someone makes a thoughtful response, the sentential wholes are much more obviously under the control of a rule that formulates itself as it goes on, as it governs the emergent sentences. The auditors have present to them not only the sentences but the thought in them, which they also achieve, in the derivative way of listeners, along with the speaker. Even the speaker himself has the thought become present to him only in its expression; it is not first completed in the mind and then expressed (although there are obviously cases in which he expressed it earlier and only repeats it now). This more lively presence of the proposition as rule is the paradigm for analysis, and the written speech should be taken as a modification of it. These remarks on writing, reading, and extemporaneous speech, incidentally, are only suggestions of the intricate ways the proposition is involved with the passage of time.

The proposition as a rule also accounts for the possibility of vagueness. Someone judging vaguely lets his sentences be formed by all the rules that govern them from "outside"—phonemic, lexical, grammatical—but is not able to let the force of the propositional rule, the one that works from "inside," take effect. That is why he is quite willing to reformulate the sentences in ways that exasperate the person who understands what is being said. The vague speaker may talk with extraordinary correctness, impressive vocabulary, and solemn style and tone, but he does not think while he speaks. His speech may be cultured but thoughtless. The proposition is not effectively at work governing his sentences, nor is it there to be expressed by them. Instead of being ruled by the proposition, the sentence emerges on the basis of association: words, phrases, and sentences that have often appeared in the context at issue are again put on parade, whether they fit or not.

Still less accurate than vagueness, however, is speech which is an emotional discharge. The associations in vagueness, although they may be partly idiosyncratic and private to the speaker, have at least some connections which are public and known to many persons: the object under discussion exercises at least an associative pull on the other items it brings to speech; and what is uttered in vagueness has at least a chance of being brought to distinctness since there is some concern with the object in such speech. The vague judger is at least trying to judge. But speech which is almost exclusively a symptom of feeling does not even have this direction toward and concern with the object, though it may have a sentential form. A listener trying to follow it as a registration or report of things would be bewildered by what is said, whereas someone trying to follow a vague speech would, rather, be exasperated. At the extreme, there may be no propositions at all in a speech wholly overcome by feeling or by psychological compulsions, and we are misguided if we "take seriously" what is said or think we have to come to terms with it and either assent or dissent. The sentences are ruled by compulsions, not by propositions, and this becomes more obvious the longer the person keeps talking; there is not even a judgment in vagueness. What is said is to be treated as a symptom, not a proposal for assent.

We have identified the proposition as a rule that governs the sentences that express it. This is only one half of its function of governance; to consider only this would be to take thinking as something only concerned with words. But thinking also has to do with being, with things we use and respond to and contemplate. To explore this dimension, we now consider the propositional rule as also governing our perceptions, registrations, and reports.

Note

1. See *Formal and Transcendental Logic*, trans. D. Cairns (The Hague: Nijhoff, 1969), §57-§58, §73 (they are also called "irreal" objectivities); also "The Origin of Geometry," in *The Crisis of European Sciences and Transcendental Phenomenology*, trans. D. Carr (Evanston: Northwestern University Press, 1970), pp. 356-57.

CHAPTER 10

The Sentence as a Signal for Propositional Achievement

Things are disclosed to us in our registrations, reports, and perceptions of them. These are all activities that we execute; how is the propositional rule related to them? How is its governance over such activities related to its governance over the sentence? The activities of disclosure, the sentence, and the proposition are all interlocking aspects of truthfulness and must be clarified in terms of one another.

(I) *Sentential parts as signals of activities.* Suppose I were to make the statement "Henry is very thin." The following interlocutors and conditions of utterance must be distinguished. (a) I meet Henry's friend Paul and make the statement as a report, because Henry is not there when I say it. Paul has not seen Henry for some time, but he simply believes what I say and expects to find Henry looking thin when he sees him on the next day. Henry does look thin when he appears, and the registration confirms my report. This is a case of a report which is accepted naively, with no propositional turn at any point. (b) I meet another friend of Henry, Jonathan, and tell him the same thing, once again as a report. But he is skeptical because he does not understand how Henry could have gotten thin, so he accepts what I say as only my proposition, my opinion. This is a report with a propositional turn. How does the sentence function in each of these cases? (To round out the description, it is also necessary to mention that we as analysts also have the proposition present to us, but we are beyond both the

credulity of Paul and the skepticism of Jonathan; we are attempting
to describe the exchange and the verification but are not engaged as
participants in it. We leave this complication aside for the moment.)

In case (a), when I tell Paul that Henry is thin, he simply goes
along with what I say in an assent-articulation. Under my guidance
he names Henry and he names the aspect of thinness. He also
articulates the two, he distinguishes and unites them, in a believing
way. His naming and articulating are activities he performs, and
they are similar to the activities I perform when I tell him the fact;
the major difference is that I am more active in the activity, because
I tell while he listens and goes along. However, our parallel activities are not arranged by some sort of preestablished harmony; they
occur together because of the words that come between us, the
words I utter in my sentence, "Henry is very thin."

These words, and the sentence as a whole, can be understood as
signals. They are signals of activities, and signals in two senses:
(1) they signal that I am executing the activities; (2) they signal to
Paul to execute his activities. The same word is a signal *of* and a
signal *to*. The concept of signal always has this double possibility,
of being either a sign that something has occurred or a sign to do
something; I can signal that I have reached the top of the hill, and I
can signal the others to follow me. In the uttered sentence, the
word "is" signals that I am articulating (with assent), and it signals
Paul to do the same. The words "Henry" and "thin" also signal;
they signal the activity of naming, and also signal a syntactical element, since one word is being used as a subject and the other as a
predicate. Paul is signalled to hold Henry as a subject and to consider him attributed as thin, and I am signalled as doing this myself.[1]

Paul hears my report while Henry is not around. He accepts it
without question and without the propositional turn. As I say it and
after I say it, Paul asserts that Henry is thin; he may repeat it to
someone else and may muse about it while he is alone. When he
does all this he names Henry, in his absence, and articulates him as
thin. All this remains in the domain of report. Then Paul finally sees
Henry; because of his conviction, he expects to register him as thin.
If this transformation of report into registration is to occur, Paul
must now name Henry in his presence and articulate him in his
presence as thin. As we have seen in chapter five, this requires that

the syntactical articulation (which he originally accepted from me) is now to be fused with the prepredicative, perceptual "taking as." Paul must not only say the words and "think the thought" in Henry's presence; he must also see Henry as thin (conversely, Henry must appear as thin), and the two levels, the predicative and the prepredicative, fuse with one another. What is "taken as" is identified with what is "said to be." Moreover, Paul expects to live through this fusion because of what I said.

Suppose Paul has not yet seen Henry and is still in the condition of reporting. How do the words function as signals? The word "is" signals an articulation (with assent, as usual). It signals an activity. The act is more than the mere achievement of the word, because the word could be thoughtlessly repeated; the activity is the thinking that is to occur with the word. Other grammatical particles or other words may have signalled the same act of thinking; for example, "has gotten," "has become," or even "has lost weight" as a substitute for "is very thin"—all these are acceptable as substitutes provided the speaker has not deliberately selected one or the other but is willing to accept them as equivalent to get across the idea of being thin. Then, as we have seen in chapter nine, the critical question is this: is the signalling word "is" related to the act of thinking the articulation in the same way as the imperative "hold your arm straight" is related to the act of holding your arm straight when you swing a golf club? We have determined that it is not. The signal in "is" signals Paul only to articulate (with assent). If he is paying attention, he does this together with achieving the word "is" and its grammatical subject and predicate. He does it while he hears me speak, he does it later when he thinks about Henry and perhaps when he says to someone else "He's gotten thin," and he does it again when he sees Henry and says "He is quite thin." These acts, although they are in one sense the same because they achieve the same fact, are subtly differentiated by being repeated in different situations: Paul first acts under my signal, he then acts as a reporter using his own signals, he finally acts as a registrar; but even when he acts as reporter and registrar his activities are modified by being repetitions of an original which I gave him. All the acts, however, hang on the signal "is" and the other signalling words of the sentence.

Of special concern is the registration. Here the articulation is supposed to find its foundation, its prepredicative, perceptual basis. Paul expects not only to say the sentence when he sees Henry, but to be able to relax the syntax and become more passive, to "take" Henry "as" thin, to let Henry appear thin. This too is a kind of doing or activity on Paul's part, and it is also under the sway of the linguistic signals I originally uttered to him. Now this prepredicative "taking as" or perceiving is related to the signal in "is" rather more the way a golf swing is related to the imperatives about how to swing. The perception is different from the syntactical articulation. Perceiving is different from thinking, "taking as" is different from "saying (and thinking) is." However, because of the intimacy between perception and registration, because the "taking as" becomes blended with the "saying is" in registration, the difference is not as sharp as that between the golf swing and the command; but there is more of a difference than between the "is" and the activity of thinking a predication.

In contrast to Paul, consider case (b), the case of the skeptical Jonathan. Paul was credulous; he articulated with me while I made my report and he never annulled his assent, even throughout his repetitions and his confirming registration. But hardly had I finished my report when Jonathan made the propositional turn. He could not see how Henry might have gotten thin, and he took what I said as only my opinion. But this turnabout is also made possible by the sentence as signal: Jonathan carries out the articulation but annuls assent; this means that he follows the signal in "is" but also, explicitly, looks at "is" as a signal. Paul just followed the signal, Jonathan also makes it thematic as a signal. This is the extra move that annuls assent; this is the modification of the naive situation that constitutes the propositional turn. The word "is" and the other parts of the sentence are taken in a new, non-standard way, and this adjusts the effect they normally and spontaneously have. Reflection on a proposition is achieved by articulating, in obedience to the signalling word, but also by focusing on the signalling word as a signal and becoming explicitly aware that one is being urged to think in this way. The loss of naivety in a critical listener *is* his becoming aware of the signal as signal, and this *is* the inhibition of assent which we have called the propositional turn. This becoming aware of the sentential signal is the modification of belief, the suppression of assent, which we have described in chapter six as the process of changing facts into propositions, into supposed facts as supposed.

In this adjustment the sentence as signal is the pivot for the propositional turn. The sounding words in their almost physical presence are there to be taken in a new way. The words and sentence become a focus of our attention in a way they were not before; when they simply affected us and made us think naively about things, our concern was with the things, and words were signals we followed but thematically overlooked. As it is often said, our attention went "through" the words to things (our explanation of words as signals is an attempt to provide the literal sense of this spatial metaphor). When we become critical we turn to words precisely as signals, and this also modifies the way we take the facts we earlier co-reported or co-registered in a naive way. Furthermore, both senses of signal are acknowledged in our new focus: because Jonathan makes the propositional turn, he sees my use of "is" as signalling that I articulate Henry as thin, so he attributes the proposition, the fact as supposed, to me as my opinion; and he also sees the "is" as signalling him to make the same assenting articulation, so he now takes the fact as a proposal I am making, as a guarantee that he will find Henry to be thin when he manages to see him again.

The signalling function of words is related primarily to the activities performed by the speaker, listener, reporter, registrar, repeater, and perceiver. We will return to this subject, but must first explore the second major dimension in the function of words, the expressive. The sentence is said to express a proposition, and earlier we have said that the sentence expresses the propositional rule that governs it. We now examine the notion of expression; it will have an effect on the final determination of the concept of words as signals.

(II) *The expressed and the named.* So long as the proposition or judgment is conceived as a mental sign or psychological entity of some sort, there is little difficulty in showing what a sentence is supposed to express: the exprimend is that mental entity, the thought. But we have defined the proposition as the fact as supposed; what is left to be expressed? We will account for expression by relating it to names, and will identify, with proper qualifications, the exprimend with what is named.[2]

When I say "Henry is thin," the words "Henry" and "thin" work as names, according to the analysis we have given in chapter three. Both words are among the standard, first-level names that name things and features. The word "is" is at first contrasted to the lexicon of the sentence; it is part of the grammar or syntax and does not name the way the other words do. However, on another level, "is" is also a name: it does not name an object or a feature, but it does name the predicational crease that arises with Henry and his thinness when he is articulated as being thin. This crease arises only in response to the activity of articulating, whether in registration or in report. Clearly it is not a thing or a feature, but it is the distinction that comes between thing and feature. The distinction could not occur unless there were the thing and its feature, but once the distinction does come about, it can be named. The thing and its feature (Henry and thin) are named by standard names, but the distinction, the predicational crease, is named by "is." True, "is" is involved in syntax and linkage, but linkage here is precisely articulation, the distinguishing of thing and feature, and the activated distinction is also named by "is."

Like all names, "is" can be used in the presence or the absence of what it names. When I report that Henry is thin, "is" names the absent crease; when I register the fact, "is" names the present crease. And the crease is recognized as being the same in presence and absence, in registration and report; the crease, and the fact it constitutes, is the same whether it is present or absent to me. Furthermore, "is" as a name is tied to the assent that normally permeates all articulation. As long as I have not moved into special discourse like that of fiction, when I name the predicational crease I imply that it is presentable at least in principle to somebody. Of course the crease is made present not by just looking at something, but by looking and thinking: by looking and predicating and hence activating the crease.

"Henry" names Henry, "thin" names his condition, and "is" names the crease between the two. We should not say, however, that the sentence "Henry is thin" names the fact that he is thin, because when we report or register we do not name the fact; we name its ingredients, but we articulate the fact. We would name it only when we nominalize what we have articulated. But we can say that the sentence expresses the fact. The fact registered or reported is the exprimend of the sentence used for the registration or report. The relationship of expression is not a relation between sentences and mental entities, but between sentences and their registered or reported facts. This is confirmed even in ordinary speech; when someone gives a good account of something, we say that his words expressed the situation or the occurrence well.

Certainly we sometimes say a speaker expressed his opinions or his judgments or thoughts well or badly; but these thoughts are simply his facts as supposed. When a critical listener like Jonathan makes the propositional turn and no longer simply co-registers or co-reports, he finds the speaker's sentences expressing the man's proposals, the facts as he presents them. More specifically, Jonathan takes the "is" uttered by the speaker in a new way: instead of allowing it to name the predicational crease, Jonathan makes it thematic as naming the crease, and he takes the crease itself only as named and activated by the speaker. Consequently, the articulated fact is not simply accepted but is considered only as proposed.

Actually, whenever we do make a remark like "His words express the situation very well," we have almost always made the propositional turn. We first thought directly about the objects and facts, then we paid attention to what the man was saying and admired it as his proposal, then we finally saw that his words were a good expression of the manifestation taking place. We performed the zig-zag motion back and forth between fact and proposal. Because we have turned to the proposition in this way, we are tempted to say the words primarily express a proposition or someone's ideas or thoughts, and we are all the more inclined to postulate the proposition as a mental entity or sign "behind" the words. We postulate as an entity something that arises only correlatively to our shift in attitude, and we tend to forget that sentences express facts and situations primarily; they express thoughts only as facts as supposed.

(III) *How the proposition can be a rule for sentences.* When I express a rule for an ordinary action, like swinging a golf club or changing a tire, I name the action; I say "hold" or "swing" or "raise (the car)." When I get someone to think along with me while I speak, I do not name his activity of thinking; I do not say "predicate." But I say "is," and this word signals the activity of predicating but does not name it; it names the predicational crease in the object under discussion. Getting someone to think along with me is something like getting him to imitate me while I swing the club or raise the car. I get him to do as I am doing, and this is the way we all begin to think at first until we can take over on our own. However, what I am doing when I express thoughts is involved with language, and both of us, I and my imitator in thinking, perform our thinking upon the single sounding speech that I speak and he hears.

But what are we, each of us, doing? We are not just thinking, we are thinking or articulating or framing this fact. We are thinking the fact which is expressed in our sentence, the fact whose ingredients are named by the linguistic elements of the sentence. The sentence and its words signal not merely that I am thinking, but that I am thinking this fact; they do not signal my interlocutor just to think, but to think this fact (there is no thinking which is not the framing of some fact; there is no sheer thinking without specification). Therefore, the sentence that signals the thinking cannot be just any sentence; it has to be a sentence that can signal the thinking of this fact. Therefore the composition of the sentence has to be regulated by the fact we are signalled to think. Therefore the sentence must be governed by the fact taken as a rule; therefore, as we said in chapter nine, the proposition is to be understood as a rule that governs the sentence by which it is expressed. The sentence is also governed by phonemic, etymological, philological, and grammatical rules, but the ultimate rule that governs its composition is the proposition, specifically the proposed fact which we are signalled to think as we hear the sentence. Clustered around the sentence, therefore, are the acts of thinking that it signals, the things, features, and creases that its words name, and the fact and the proposition that it expresses and by which it is governed.

The sentence is governed by the proposition, not by the fact registered or reported with the sentence. It is only when the fact is taken as supposed or proposed that it becomes a rule for sentences, because only then does it take on the modality of suggesting what people ought to say when they utter sentences. To be a rule for sentences, the fact has to become imposed by someone; the directing force of the rule has to have a director behind it who is responsible for showing what ought to be said. It is the fact as proposed by someone that governs sentences.

"But this fact as proposed is surely in turn measured by the fact pure and simple, the fact we register and report. Does this not make the fact itself into a rule, one that governs the propositional rule and subsequently the sentence?" True, the proposition is measured by the fact pure and simple. A speaker, if he is honest and responsible, cannot make any propositions he feels like making; he must articulate what is the case. But the fact pure and simple (not as proposed) should not be called a rule: it does not carry along with itself the sense that someone is reporting or registering it, or that it should be reported or registered and so govern what is said. The fact is disclosed as just there. But when the fact is taken as proposed, the sense that someone proposes it, and that it is proposed to someone, and that it therefore is to be expressed in a certain way in a sentence, becomes a dimension of the fact; indeed, this is what the "fact as proposed" means. There is an element of ruling and guidance which requires someone to be the ruler and guide over what is to be uttered in speech. This element is not present in the disclosure of a fact, in the manifestation of being; being is not a ruler, nor is it a somebody responsible for guidance; it is just there with its necessity and truth, which is more an invitation to acceptance rather than a directive. Being and its disclosure measure the proposition, which in turn rules language, but being and its disclosure do not rule the proposition, because they do not work as a ruling power. Only when the disclosure of being, a fact, becomes appropriated and attached to someone as a proposal does it turn into a ruling force over language. The intervening of a speaker between being or facts and what everyone says is the emergence of a ruling power that brings with itself the dimensions of signalling, various levels of rhetoric, teaching, and dialectics, as well as sophistry and deceit and chatter. This intervention between being and what everyone says has been called *Dasein* by Heidegger; its emergence is constituted by the various processes of naming, executing syntax, indicating, taking as, and the other themes we have examined in this book, as well as by temporality and other structures and activities.

Facts measure propositions, but they do not govern them; nor do they govern the use of language in sentences. As we have seen in chapter one, we can register a fact even in the evocative use of language, in which our words can be highly idiosyncratic and devoid of accurate syntax; only when the need arises to hold sway over what others are to say and understand, and over what we ourselves are to repeat later, only when we move toward explicit description and reporting, do we have to be more definite in our linkage and say more precisely what we want said. We then strengthen the propositional as we magnify our influence over the speech of others, and what we say becomes more vividly a rule for the sentences wé express it in. Most of our lives are lived amid the governance of propositions and in the element of language, within what "they" say about things; but there are times when what is said is returned to what is the case for verification and correction, and there are times when what is said and proposed becomes established for the first time as someone has the insight to let things speak for themselves. Truth occurs as both the confirmation and the establishment of what is to be said. The awesome dominance of what "they" say must not make us think that meanings or proposals, without truth, are all that there is.

The difference between the way facts measure propositions and the way propositions rule sentences is brought out in the case of perceptual verification. In verification we go from a proposition to a registered fact, but, as we have seen, we must go beyond the articulated fact into the prepredicative, de-syntaxed "taking as" that underlies the fact. If the proposition is to be confirmed as true, Jonathan must not only *say* Henry is thin when he sees him, he must be able to take Henry as thin, or let him appear as thin. As we have seen, a proposition is also a rule for perceptions. It encourages us to try to see the object as the proposition articulates it, and more or less guarantees that we will be able to let the object appear as described. When we actually perceive the object and try to articulate it according to our expectation, we may find that the object resists our attempt. Henry does not appear as thin but as chubby.

This resistance to our articulation is not the force of another rule asserting itself in Henry as we see him, a rule urging us to take him as chubby. It is not a conflict of two opinions, not a conflict of two rules. Henry just is chubby; he is perceived as chubby and we can take it or leave it, but the measure is there. A measure does not urge the way a rule does. There is nothing rhetorical about a fact; facts do not need to persuade us, they do not care whether or not we measure up to them in what we say.

The analyses we have completed in this chapter have brought a kind of closure to our treatment of propositions. We have shown how propositions serve to rule sentences and how they guide perceptions; we have insisted that propositions are measured by facts but that it is wrong to say facts are rules; we have discussed sentences as signals of the activity of thinking and have related the naming function of sentences to their expressive activity; and we have related the sentential signals to the propositional turn. Many of the statements made in earlier chapters find their explanation in these analyses. The pivot in the activities we here describe is the sentence: how it is taken determines whether we have a fact or a supposition, and our very activity of thinking is attached to the words that make up the sentence. The public, vocal character of the sentence and its parts assures us that neither the proposition nor facts are private, hidden, or psychological things. They are public achievements done with words that are sounded out loud. The mind which does all this is also a public reality, not something private and inaccessible, and its activities are public and so are its effects. Many more clarifications concerning the proposition and its related topics remain to be made and many implications must still be drawn out; we cannot cover all of these, but some will be treated in the remainder of this chapter.

(1) *Verification.* Confirming or denying a proposition, deciding by observation whether it is true or not, does not involve comparing a proposition with a registered fact, as though they were two objects that are to be found similar or isomorphic to each other. Rather, verification involves annulling the propositional turn (which was itself a modification of an original naive belief). We go back to the object and reregister what we have just supposed. We again carry out the same categorial or syntactic performances we executed in

our disengaged, propositional way, and we now remember having held it as only propositional. The new registration is recognized as confirming what was held as a proposal. We do not return to our original naivety, for the propositional restraint has intervened and modifies the new, confirming registration. The strength of our belief is increased by such criticism, and if someone raises the same issue again as a question or a proposition, we would say we assent to what he formulates. We would say that what he says "is true." On the other hand, after taking the propositional turn we may return to the things and find that we cannot reregister what we did before. What we "take" the thing "as" perceptually is recalcitrant to the categorial forms and names we try to fuse with it. We approach the chair ready to say it is brown—that is the way we saw it in the dim light yesterday—but it can now only be taken as a shade of gray. The proposition "This chair is brown" is still a proposition, but it is one we dissent from, one we would say is false. Our mind is littered with many such propositions which we no longer hold, but which we could still formulate as beliefs we once had.

Once we have become accustomed to turning from naive agreement to the propositional attitude, and then back again to objects for confirmation or rejection, it becomes possible for us to turn any remark into a mere proposition. This is not true only for remarks others make; we can take what we say ourselves as a proposition in order to see whether our belief is well grounded. Because sentential utterances accompany registrations and reports, they are available to be contemplated as signals, making what we say only a proposal; we always "overhear" what we say ourselves and we can become critical toward it. The possibility of a propositional turn is always on the margin of any report or registration; conversely, whenever we take what is said propositionally, the possibility of returning to registration and report is marginally there. The only reason we take it propositionally is to go back to things and confirm or deny what is proposed. Because these possibilities of changes in attitude are always reciprocally marginal to one another, the illusion arises that there are two radically different things available: a fact as a condition of objects, and a proposition as a psychological entity. The dependence of each on the attitude we take is overlooked. The two, fact and proposition, are erroneously made into two entities which "are there" before we turn to them, entities which solicit our attention and reflection. This is the typical philosophical mistake of making an independent thing out of something that is a moment dependent on something else. We are tempted to make the proposition a thing to which we can turn in reflection, as though it were there before we changed our attitude, and as though we had to add our assent to it. But the proposition arises when we change the way we take facts, and it is dependent on our "turn toward" it.

The illusion of two separate things, proposition and fact, leads to a badly formulated correspondence theory of truth, in which the proposition is somehow to be mapped on to a fact. There is a sense in which the proposition does correspond to a fact, but only through the shifts of attitude that characterize going from one to the other: we can formulate something as a proposition, then formulate it, in registration, as a fact, with the awareness of identity in the two achievements. What we now register is the same as what we earlier proposed. No further act of comparing one to the other is needed. The confirming registration itself identifies what it registers with what was supposed.

(2) *Two excesses as regards propositions.* There are two extremes in the attitude people have to what is said. Some listeners are gullible and go along with every report and registration they hear. For them, speech is compelling. They do not have much of a sense of the propositional; everything said—and perhaps more frequently, everything written—is carried out in concord. This is the way children first speak and use language, before they come to discriminate between what is and what is said to be, and it is characteristic of childlike speakers. At the other extreme there are persons who have become so critical or so suspicious that they hardly ever go along with a report or registration. They trip up almost any remark, even those that are meant to be casual and noncontroversial, the harmless statements that keep human contact and sympathy alive. Everything is put into the propositional state and nothing is given assent. This is the extreme of Plato's misologist:

If there were in fact a true and solid discourse (*logos*) that could be known, what a lamentable condition it would be if a

man, because he ran into the kind of speeches (*logoi*) we have
mentioned, which seemed to be true at one time and not at
another, would not blame himself or his own lack of skill, but
finally, because of his distress, be glad to shift the blame from
himself to what is said (*epi tous logous*), and for the rest of his
life persist in hating and vilifying all discussions (*tous logous*),
and so be deprived of the truth and knowledge of things.
(*Phaedo* 90C-D; see 89C-91C)

Even this sort of man could become what he is only on the basis of
earlier agreements and reports and registrations done in concord
with others; and if pushed far enough in his present skeptical condition, he would have to concede, at least by what he cannot avoid
doing in his actions or in the intellectual moves he makes, that
there are some things he not only entertains as propositions, but
actually believes.

(3) *The propositional rule and the activity of disclosure.* Taking
the proposition as a rule emphasizes the fact that the manifestation
of things, registration, reporting, perceiving, and the like, are all
aspects of an activity, of something that happens between things
and their datives of manifestation, of something that must be carried out. The activity of disclosure must not be confused with processes like spatial or chemical changes, actions like political or
social achievements, or productions like making tables. Moreover,
we must not duplicate the activities: we do not have manifestation
happening in things and, say, registration as something different
occurring in people; manifestation and registration, or manifestation and perception, are one activity described from different an-
gles. Furthermore, the activity of disclosure has various structures
and permits various achievements. Besides registration, reporting,
and perception, there are things like quotation, attribution of opinions, facts being nominalized, things being "taken as" this or that,
questions and answers, and picturing. All these things happen as
different kinds of manifestation, different forms of truthfulness, and
to analyze their structures is one of the functions of philosophy.

Many kinds of disclosure, many forms of being "taken as," can
occur before language, but speech allows us to regulate manifestation and to carry out more penetrating identifications. One way in

which this occurs is through the regulation that propositional rules exercise over our perceptions and expectations. Such proposals had to be formulated by someone at some time; perceptive persons register important truths, and establish sayings that help others articulate things as they really are. There is a kind of guidance exercised by some minds over the perceptions and the discourse of others, but if the propositions in question are true and helpful, we are indebted to those who first formulated them; they illuminate our world and our actions in it.

Like all performances, the activity of disclosure can be done first in a passive, imitative way. We simply do what everyone else does and may not even recognize that our activity can be improved by rules (just as we might swing a golf club in imitation of someone else without knowing the principles that would allow us to do it better). Things are disclosed to us before we talk about them. But the emergence of speech brings these disclosures to a more perfect and reliable state. And even if our own use of speech is passive and vague at the beginning, it is the start of our own thinking and our own ability to register and disclose things. We become truthful gradually, not out of sheer ignorance and silence. Furthermore, although the prepredicative ways of "taking" things "as" this or that may be more vague than explicit registrations, they are nonetheless more elementary and original. The proposition, the rule for sentences and further perceptions, is derived from and measured by them; the proposition can govern our discourse and our perceptions only because it originates in the disclosure of things.

(4) *Peculiarities of the propositional rule.* Rules that govern ordinary actions can be formulated in two ways, in either the hypothetical or the imperative mode. I can say "If you want to change the tire, raise the car, etc.," and "If you want to swing the club properly, turn your hand more to the left." I can also say simply "Raise the car" and "Turn your hand farther this way." In the case of the proposition as rule, there are not two distinct formulations available. I always say simply "Henry has become thin." However, depending on how my statement is taken, analogues to the hypothetical and the imperative modes can be found in the proposition. If my interlocutor makes the propositional turn, he takes what I say in

something of a hypothetical manner: he takes my statement as a suggestion of what he and others should say if they want to tell the truth, and what they should expect to see if they want to be prepared for things as they are. This hypothetical element is not expressed in any part of the sentence, but it is part of the sense of what we have present to us when we make the propositional turn. On the other hand, someone who listens naively and submissively to what I say, without the propositional turn, reacts to my words as to imperatives. What I say has no sense of the conditional or the merely proposed for him.

Neither the hypothetical nor the imperative aspect is explicitly expressed in the words that formulate the proposition; I do not say "If you want to tell the truth, say Henry is thin," nor do I say "Say Henry is thin." Both aspects are part of the structural sense of the proposition, however, and when we get into the more external actions of changing tires or playing sports or cooking food, the two modes acquire distinct expressive forms. In our exposition, we have used the rules for external actions as models to get to the structure of propositional rules; the rules for external actions were "first for us." However, although it is more difficult to analyze, the propositional rule is "first in itself" and can be seen as the origin for the rules governing external behavior. The two explicit and expressed modes, the hypothetical and the imperative, are derived from the structural possibilities of the propositional and are conditioned by it. It is only because we are capable of executing the intimate activities of understanding and thinking along with what people say that we are able to follow rules of behavior that are expressed in words.

A final question may be raised to close this chapter. We say that a proposition is true or false, but we do not say that a rule is true or false. If the proposition is to be considered a rule, how can it be true or false? The interlocutors who propose and accept a proposition are not the ones who call it a rule; they consider it a proposal and they say it is true or false. We as philosophical analysts contemplate propositions and we say they are rules that govern certain activities and sentential compositions. The activities are executed by the interlocutors, by Paul and Jonathan and the person speaking to them. We ourselves are not in the business of affirming or denying the propositions in question; we take them as affirmed, denied, or proposed by the interlocutors. When we analyze what it is for a proposition to be true for them, we show the sequence of activities they must achieve and we consider the proposition as regulating these activities. The interlocutors do not examine the activities, even though they execute them; they merely say the statement is true or false, but we show how they are able to say that. By calling a proposition a rule we are able to explain what it is for the interlocutors to say that a proposition is true or false. We as philosophical analysts call the proposition a rule; the interlocutors do not do so. And since they, not we, are the ones who say a particular statement is true or false, our analysis does not lead to the necessity of saying that a rule is true or false. To make this claim would be to confuse the prephilosophical with the philosophical viewpoint.

Notes

1. My concept of signalling is developed from Husserl's description of words as indication signs (*Anzeichen*) of acts of thinking; see *Logical Investigations*, trans. J. N. Findlay (New York: Humanities Press, 1970), Investigation I, §2-§3, §7-§8, §25.

2. Husserl observes that it is incorrect to say an expression expresses its sense or meaning, because an expression is a whole which includes meaning as one of its parts; he goes on to say that an expression should be taken to express the object or states of affairs we intend through the expression; see *Logical Investigations*, Investigation I, §10-§15; Investigation VI, §4, §8. Also *Cartesian Meditations*, trans. D. Cairns (The Hague: Nijhoff, 1960), §4 par. 6, §5 par. 5.

CHAPTER 11

Four Series of Refinements

Several series of distinctions can now be made to clarify points that have been left obscure, to draw relationships between elements we have described in isolation, and to reinforce some distinctions we have drawn. The first series concerns the kinds of sounds a human being can make.

(1) A person has not spoken until he has been understood. If he makes syntactical signals, the interlocutor must respond to them and co-perform the syntactical activity they signal. But even more fundamentally, the interlocutor must appreciate that the person before him is trying to speak or signal; he must take him as engaged in discourse. There are many other kinds of sounds he might be making which do not involve linguistic signalling. First, there are noises like coughs, sneezes, snores, and burps, which do not involve the larynx but do require motion of the diaphragm. Then there are sounds like groans, laughs, screams, and purrs, which require the activity of the vocal cords but are not articulated by the tongue and lips. Third, there are interjections like "ouch," "well, well," and "oh," which are both voiced and articulated—hence they can be quoted, while the first two kinds could only be named—but which do not name anything and do not enter into syntax. These interjections, which we might call expletives, are emitted as the effect of emotion, pain, surprise, or some other internal condition of the speaker, and are not primarily addressed to anyone. If the pain, pleasure, or shock is in turn caused by some object, like a fire or an

unexpected cool breeze on a hot day, the sounds can be considered symptoms of the objects as well as of one's feelings. But, fourth, there are other interjections, like "hello," "hey," "say," or perhaps the listener's name, which are used to establish contact with an interlocutor or audience; no emotion or shock need provoke them, and they too stand outside the grammar of any sentence. Fifth, we must distinguish, from the two kinds of interjections we have just mentioned, still another kind, the exclamations we have discussed in chapter four. Cries like "ouch" are a symptom of a disturbance in me but do not necessarily draw attention to anything common, and words like "hello" are directed toward the interlocutor in making contact with him but do not refer to any subject to be spoken about. They introduce no "third" person or thing. Exclamations, like "look out," alert the hearer to something prominent, so they do more than establish contact; however, they do not specify what the intruding object is, and have nothing to say about it.

Properly linguistic activity involves initiating and articulating sounds that both name things and combine variously with one another: the sounds are words with lexicon and grammar. The auditor must appreciate the sounds as being controlled—initiated and shaped—by the speaker. He takes them as words, and thereby recognizes the presence of the speaker who is controlling them. Words and sentences, besides playing a crucial role in the shift from fact to proposition, are also the medium which, when taken properly, announces the presence of a speaker. The auditor recognizes the words because he achieves them along with the speaker; there is only one sounding voice, and the spoken/heard words are accomplished by the speaker and the hearer, one leading and the other following.[1]

We have progressed through noises, voiced sounds, expletives, sounds achieving contact, exclamations, and words and sentences. In the last item, the presence of a speaker is also achieved. As the final state in this series, the auditor can also appreciate the thought of the speaker, if indeed he does speak intelligently. The auditor does this by obeying the grammatical signals the speaker makes and by articulating the facts or framing the propositions along with him: not by doing something separate from hearing the words, but by using the spoken words—which are simultaneously his own heard words—as the expressive support for his own activity of thinking. The auditor can turn even more directly toward the speaker by making the propositional turn. As long as he simply goes along registering or reporting with the speaker, he takes what is said simply as the way things are, and the peculiar authority of the speaker is not pushed to the fore. But if the auditor takes the remarks as proposals—by turning in still another way toward the words made by the speaker and considering them explicitly *as* signals of thought—the proposition is taken as what this man is saying, and his ability and responsibility become a direct issue.

As in the case of fact and proposition, it is important to avoid philosophical duplication in the case of the speaker and the auditor, particularly in regard to words and sentences. It is not true that the speaker makes and also overhears one sentence, which then turns into sound waves that strike the other man's ear, where new sounds similar to the first are engendered and another sentence is achieved, one similar in type to that of the speaker. This picture conceives of minds as isolated from one another and aware only of stimuli affecting the body. But minds are public, present to one another and aware of things, minds are intentional, as Husserl called them; and they are able to operate simultaneously on one voiced speech, heard both by the speaker himself and by his auditor. The single sentence is recognized by both minds. It is further recognized and identified by someone who carries out a philosophical analysis of the process of speaking, but his identification is parasitic on that of the original interlocutors, which must come first. He acknowledges what they have achieved.

These various possibilities of uttered sounds should not be confused with one another. Quine, for example, considers "ouch" to be a simple sentence, but he fails to distinguish between words and caused symptoms of pleasure, pain, shock, and the like; in this view, no distinction is permitted between the achievement of someone addressing us and the whimpering of a beast or the burps and grunts of some Caliban-like creature.[2]

(2) A second series of distinctions concerns various ways of detaching our agreement from what is said. The unmodified form of hearing someone speak is naive acceptance. I as listener simply go along with what the speaker says and derivatively report or register facts with him. It does not occur to me to question anything or to

suspend my belief. When I make the propositional turn, I consider the fact as merely proposed or supposed by the speaker, but many levels are possible here. I may take the proposal as the opinion of the particular individual who expressed it; or I may take it as a general, floating opinion that is commonly held now, like some widespread conviction about politics or sports that is in the air at the present time; or, more attenuated still, I can take it as an opinion that not many people formulate explicitly, but that they would assent to if the proposition were put to them. (For example: "Should people have freedom of speech in New Zealand?" "Of course." Public opinion polls operate with this third sort of proposition, although they claim to be measuring something that straddles the first two: the explicit opinions of individuals, or the ideas commonly held by most people. And there is a difference; propositions that people do not disagree with, or propositions they might agree with when someone puts a question to them, are not necessarily proposals they would make themselves.) Finally, at the extreme, I may find that a certain proposition is tautologous and must be admitted by anyone who understands it. Such variations in attributing a proposition are not recognized when we naively register or report facts while others are articulating them, because the speaker does not come to the fore as an issue until we turn, at least marginally, from the facts to the propositions and to the one who proposes them.

In the cases we have listed, I as listener acknowledge that either certain individuals or "everybody" assents to the proposition in question even though I may only entertain it as a proposal at the time. There are negative correlates to the four cases we have described; in them I disaffiliate a proposition from speakers in different ways: I can recognize a proposition as denied by an individual, as denied by "everybody," or as a proposal people would deny if they were asked about it. Finally, again at the extreme, I can determine that what is put together in an expression is not a consistent or coherent sense at all, and so could not be asserted by anyone who uttered it thoughtfully, with distinctness and clarity. This is the opposite to a tautology.

In both the positive and the negative cases we have surveyed, we have dealt with the turn to propositions. It is also possible to make a "sentential turn," with a new kind of detachment from belief. A sentence found as an example in a book of grammar, a sentence contrived to illustrate the use of a word or a grammatical form, a sentence spoken in an exercise while I am learning a new language, these are not sentences used to express propositions. They and all the grammatical moves in them are dummies which do not signal any propositional or syntactic achievements. When sentences are used to express propositions, as we have seen, some grammatical moves may be replaceable by others with no propositional change: normally, "within a week," "before the end of a week," "by week's end" would be equivalent; but as samples of grammar they differ from one another. Therefore, when sentences are not used for the ulterior purpose of expressing propositions, all the grammatical moves in them are significant and one form cannot readily be substituted for another. Furthermore, since the sentence is not being ruled by any speaker, and no one is taking any position with the sentence, we cannot appeal to anyone's intention to determine whether two different grammatical forms are equivalent or not. The individuality of each sentence comes to the fore when the sentence is an end in itself. In this case, there is really nothing calling for assent or dissent, since no proposition is achieved. I do not commit myself to anything when I make practice moves in rehearsing a new language; only after I acquire some facility in it do I trust myself enough to use it for statements. Therefore it is possible for us to achieve a sentence without achieving a proposition, and to achieve a proposition—as held by someone else, or by people in general—without achieving a fact.

(3) A third series of distinctions deals with signalling and rhetoric in speech. The most complete exercise of rhetoric takes place in a full discourse, normally composed of many sentences. A rhetorical composition is designed by the speaker to bring about assent in his audience in regard to matters that could be determined in various ways. The issues are imprecise and allow two or more alternatives. The rhetorician deals with things we are encouraged to perform, with deciding whether or not someone committed a certain action in the past, and with praising or blaming what people have done; he attempts to persuade others in regard to such matters, and uses various strategies in organizing his argument, presenting his own

character in the speech, and attempting to move the emotions of his listeners in a way that will lead them to agree with him.

This is rhetoric on its full scale. But in a diminished form, it functions also in the selection of grammatical parts of a sentence. We have seen that the conjunction "but" can be reduced to "and" in respect to its truth value. The truth tables of both are the same: "He came but he did not stay" is true under exactly the same conditions as "He came and he did not stay." However, the use of "but" looks to the listener and to the expectations aroused in his mind by the first part of the sentence; the speaker knows a particular anticipation will be provoked by "he came," and he explicitly counteracts and cancels it by adding "but" to the final part, "he did not stay." The selection of "but" instead of "and" could be called a rhetorical choice. It is made with the auditor, not the truth conditions of the statement, in mind. The selection of "however," "nevertheless," "still," and "yet" in place of "and" provides further examples. A rich profusion of such grammatical possibilities exists because the moves the mind can make in responding to what is said are so varied: suspicion, enthusiastic acceptance, royal disdain, expectation of particular consequences, expectation of certain kinds of denials, non-expectation of other consequences. Some moves, like that involved with "but," may be so common that almost all languages will have some way of expressing them; others may be rather sophisticated or unusual, or perhaps connected to peculiar social conditions and relationships found in certain communities, and they may be institutionalized in some languages and not in others. A sense for such idiosyncratic grammatical possibilities is even more important in mastering a language than learning its vocabulary.

It is appropriate to call the selection of such grammatical forms a rhetorical process. The speaker makes these selections to make it more comfortable for his audience to achieve the beliefs he is expressing. He anticipates their expectations, counters possible confusions, displays the parts of his discourse in a pleasing, rhythmic sequence in which it is easy to make the indicated distinctions and yet hold everything together in a continuous whole. The grammatical accommodation is directed not toward an action or decision subsequent to the speech—that is the work of rhetoric in its primary sense—but toward getting the speech effectively into the minds of the listeners. Grammatical rhetoric attempts to persuade the audience to achieve, with clarity and conviction, the propositions of the speech, not anything beyond the speech itself.

Finally, on a more intimate level than the rhetoric in grammar, there is the process of signalling. Grammatical forms in sentences signal achievements in the syntax of propositions. They signal that the speaker achieves the syntax, if he speaks thoughtfully, and they simultaneously signal the hearer to perform the propositional move himself. The one grammatical achievement signals in both directions. It would not be fitting to call this signalling a rhetorical achievement, because it does not involve persuading or cajoling the hearer in any way. It is a more elementary process. It underlies any attempt at persuasion. It functions in achieving the parts of a proposition as a condition for the proposition as a whole. It involves simply engaging the listener, establishing him as a listener and me as a speaker. This signalling moves us out of the darkness of noise into the first light of language, by which things are illumined and distinguished; it occurs when we realize that someone is trying to talk to us about something. Only within this setting can the strategies of persuasion, the moves of rhetoric, be initiated. This signalling moment in speech is a condition for the rhetorical: not necessarily as a stage chronologically prior to it, but as a level beneath it in the dimensions of the use of language. The rhetorical can never persuade someone to follow sounds as signals; it must presuppose that this is already being done. It is, of course, an adjustment on this level of grammatical signalling, in the way a signal is taken, that constitutes the move from registering and reporting facts naively with the speaker to accepting them only as his opinions.

(4) Our fourth and last series of distinctions deals with the way prepositions are used. In Latin and Greek, and in languages derived from them, prepositions were originally adverbs, and they still appear as such when they are parts of compound verbs. A compound verb is not the result of joining a preposition to a verb; it is a word in which the adverbial modification is not yet detached. A verb, as we have seen, names a manifestation, and adverbs bring out further aspects of the phenomenon being named. If the sense of

these adverbs requires completion, they may govern a noun. It then becomes possible for the verb to govern more cases and objects, and to do so without ambiguity, since the central sense of the verb can take one object, and the adverbial, modifying sense another. The energy of the verb is, so to speak, siphoned off into various directions. The adverbial modifier, since it now becomes attached to the noun it governs, can be pulled away from the verb and identified primarily with its own object. It ceases to be an "adverb" and becomes a "preposition," a word "placed before" another word (this name is misleading, since many prepositions may come after the word they govern). In English, for example, the word "out" is predominantly an adverb, but on some few occasions it becomes a noun-fast preposition, as in "out the window" or "out the door." We can easily imagine this usage expanding and allowing the word to become a standard preposition. The adverbial origins of prepositions leave a "naming" dimension in them: prepositions are not sheer grammatical particles whose entire sense is exhausted in their function of linking other words. They also enjoy what we have called the lexical dimension of words, and they name things, in the qualifying, supplementary way that adverbs name.

Once a word has become a preposition, its lexicographic journey is not finished. Most prepositions have gone through three senses, spatial, temporal, and causative, and many retain elements of all three senses in their current usage: "He stood by the table," "Return it by four o'clock," and "The letter was written by him." Interesting variations are possible in such development; although "by" has a German cognate in "*bei*," and although both share the same spatial sense, German has evolved other prepositions for the temporal and causative meanings. One would say, for example, "Der Brief wurde von mir geschrieben," using the preposition with the spatial sense of "coming out of me" or "coming from me," rather than one with the sense of being near, as in English. The adverbial origin behind both lines of development is obvious.

Prepositions move through their three categories of sense by metaphorical transformations. The first sense is the spatial, since spatial relationships, processes, and aspects of phenomena are the most public, most noticeable, and easiest to name. The spatial words are then metaphorically applied to temporal relationships, processes, and aspects, which are harder to identify because some of their elements and members may not be present now but available only in memory. In fact, the projection of a spatial relation onto a temporal sequence may force us to pull into memory the absent member; the metaphorical intrusion of space into time urges us to become adept at establishing fixed points in time and in our memory. An analogous development occurs in respect to anticipating the future. Finally, we can move by a further metaphorical change from *post hoc* to *propter hoc*, and attribute agency or causation or responsibility by the use of prepositions. Even here the adverbial origin is still at work, because it is usually the phenomenon named by the verb which is said to be brought about by the noun the preposition governs: "The letter *was written* by me," "He *was saved* through the surgeon's skill."

There is another use of prepositions which is qualitatively different from the three we have surveyed. In using prepositions in a spatial, temporal, and causal sense, the speaker retains a kind of naivety which is broken by the usage we will now examine. In none of these three uses has the speaker looked upon the objects and facts he is concerned with *as* objects and facts that he has articulated. He has simply accepted objects, manifestations, and various relationships, and named and articulated them. But now let us suppose he looks at one of the facts he has registered and says, "The blue color was predicated *of* the shirt," or "The blue color was attributed *to* the shirt." He uses prepositions in this remark, but they no longer fit into any of the three categories we have described. Instead of articulating a new fact, the speaker has moved "inside" one of the facts he earlier registered and has made a comment about a relationship that exists not between things but between, specifically, parts or moments of a fact, between the object and the attribute. The speaker now makes things thematic as having been articulated into object and attribute. He looks at what thinking has done and speaks about what he discovers; the naivety of a concern with things *tout court* is overcome.

In contrast to spatial, temporal, and causative senses of prepositions, let us call this the "reflective" use of a preposition. In it a preposition is used to name relations in the "space" established, by thinking, between an object and its attribute or a subject and its predicate or even a noun and its verb: we are said to predicate "of," attribute "to," say this "about" that, use a subject or object or noun "with" its predicate or attribute or verb, and find a predicate or attribute "in" its subject or object. As we have implied by our choice of examples, the reflective use of prepositions can function whether we remain concerned with things and hence speak of object and attribute, whether we make a propositional turn and speak of subject and predicate, or whether we make a grammatical turn and speak of noun and verb. The important element is that we begin to focus upon the distinctions and combinations that earlier uses of language have actualized in things.

Certain advances in the development of language are necessary to permit this reflective use of prepositions to occur. It could hardly happen in a language which is still primarily gerundial, in which continuous masses and not objects and their manifestations are registered. Even when a language comes to articulate discrete objects through the noun form, and begins to distinguish verbs from nouns, another move is required to make this distinction—of object versus attribute, subject versus predicate, noun versus verb—thematic; at that point in the development of the language, the move is waiting to be made and almost certainly will be made, but it is nevertheless a new step and requires a metaphorical transformation in the use of words that had previously been employed simply as names of things. In fact, this reflective move is, in a way, teleologically necessary. As long as language merely talks about things, it leaves out of consideration something that is inevitably "there": its own work on things, the actuality in things that it brings about itself, the truthfulness of things. This gap calls for closure, and so the passage from spatial, temporal, and causative senses to the reflective sense of prepositions is bound to be made. Once there is language there will sooner or later be grammarians and logicians.

But grammarians and logicians are not yet philosophers, and the reflective use of prepositions is not yet a philosophical use of language. Philosophy arises in a further step. Once we have moved from the spatial, temporal, and causal sense of prepositions to the reflective, there arises the problem of relating what is named by the last of these, the reflective, with what is named by the first three. How is the work of language on things to be located "somewhere,"

how is it to occur "at some time," how is it achieved "by someone"?
How is the truth of things to be integrated into the world of space,
time, and causality? The reflective use of prepositions is in-
sufficient here, because it is one of the elements to be integrated;
we must talk precisely about what this usage achieves, and so must
raise ourselves "above" it; an ulterior reflection is necessary. At this
level we shall speak of the "philosophical" use of prepositions; in a
variant on Husserl's terminology, we can speak of the way prepositions are used in transcendentalese.

The use of prepositions on this level is often misunderstood because of a tendency to take them in one of the first three senses, as
ordinary spatial, temporal, or causal terms. For example, Plato uses
prepositions in the philosophical sense when he says the Forms are
"outside" (*chōris*) things, that things are generated "in" the substrate, that the slave boy remembers what he learned "in" or "during" some other time (*Parmenides* 130C, *Timaeus* 50D, *Meno* 86A).
When the philosophical use of such prepositions is deliberately
projected into an ordinary spatial, temporal, or causative sense, we
have the elements of a philosophical myth. Since the philosophical
sense has been reached by a series of metaphorical transformations
of the preposition, it is easy enough to resuscitate one of the latent
mundane meanings of the word and to exploit its mundane implications to fabricate a story. This process, so well used by Plato, is an
"unmetaphored" use of words whose proper philosophical sense
was reached by metaphor. It reflects the subtle relationship philosophy itself—and what it talks about—has to the world investigated
by science, the crafts, and ordinary opinion. However, when a
Platonic story is heard by someone without an appreciation of the
philosophical dimension that is mirrored in it, it appears fanciful
and paradoxical. The same reaction occurs when sentences in
straight philosophical discourse (without projection into myth) are
heard without philosophical understanding. Prepositions in them
are interpreted spatially, temporally, causally, or at best
reflectively, and the statements appear contradictory or nonsensi-
cal, or they seem to be naive, misguided attempts at science. The
doctrine of substance, for example, becomes a pincushion theory,
and the impressions things make on us become psychic objects
themselves. It would be interesting to determine whether there

ever was a philosophical dilemma which was not the result of such a mistaken interpretation of philosophical terms.

We have discussed Plato, but others too use the preposition in this philosophical way: in his treatment of substance and predication, for example, Aristotle makes use of the Greek preposition *kata*, which denotes a downward motion when used with the dative and a motion "alongside" something when used with the accusative. Something is said "of" something (*ti kata tinos legetai*), some things are said "in themselves" (*kath'hauto, kata seauto*), while some are said "of something other" than themselves (*kat'allo*). Still other things are said of what is only coincidental to them (*kata sumbebēkos*). The sense of *kata* in such phrases is of decisive importance in what Aristotle means by substance, and the translation of the prepositions is the hardest part of putting his text into English. Another preposition used philosophically by Aristotle is *pros*, "toward," which he uses as a name for the category of relation and which he employs in his doctrine of the analogous use of words; still another is *ek*, "of" or "from," which is used to state that composite substance is "of" matter and form. Other examples in Aristotle and in other philosophers can easily be found. Statements using such prepositions are bound to be misunderstood if the prepositions are taken in their ordinary spatial, temporal, or causative sense.

The philosophical use of prepositions is not the absolutely final stage in this development of their usage. One further step is necessary. Just as philosophical discourse is needed to show how the achievement of language, the actualization of the truth of things, can be integrated with the world of space, time, and causation, so also the achievement of philosophy itself has to be integrated with that world and with the truthfulness accomplished by the arts, sciences, and ordinary opinions in it. We might call the turn to this inquiry the move into the metaphilosophical. To summarize then, we find prepositions used on the following four levels: (1) in spatial, temporal, and causal senses (there are metaphorical transformations even among these three); (2) in a reflective sense; (3) in a philosophical sense; (4) in a metaphilosophical sense, in what might be called the philosophy of philosophy, first philosophy, or—to use Husserl's term—the phenomenology of phenomenology.

Why have we chosen prepositions as the "part of speech" to be followed from ordinary usage to reflective, philosophical, and metaphilosophical employment? All parts of language become transformed in moving through these levels of use, and nouns, verbs, or adjectives might also have been examined. There is an advantage in selecting one class of word form instead of treating the language as a whole, because the shifts of meaning and use can be more explicitly shown; but is there any special advantage in selecting prepositions?

Prepositions are employed to name relations, and hence they have a more vivid new sense in the subsequent levels of language use. When we move up the scale we begin to make thematic certain relations which were established and functioning on the lower levels but which were not named and not made the center of focus. On the reflective level, for example, we name the relationship of predication, which was established but not made thematic in speech about things in their spatial, temporal, and causal relationships. Predication would not be one of these relations. On the reflective level, we use prepositions such as "of," "about," "in," and *kata* to name the relations we become concerned with. Then on the philosophical level we begin to name relations such as the appearance "of" objects "to" a dative of manifestation, the synthesis of a series of appearances "in" an object, the continuation of experiences "with" one another in the flow of awareness, and the belief we have "in" the world. Metaphilosophy involves naming still other relations and makes use of prepositions with yet another new sense. When we move up this scale and begin to make these relations thematic, the things related in them, the relata, also appear in a new light—they are identified within a new set of differences—and the words used to name them also acquire a new dimension of meaning. The change in prepositions is more explicit, however, and introduces more obvious novelty, so they are especially suitable for illuminating the moves from one stage to the next.

Notes

1. See Leslie H. Farber, *The Ways of the Will: Essays Toward a Psychology and Psychopathology of Will* (New York: Basic Books, 1966), p. 145: "Actually, in listening we speak the other's words. Or, to put it in another way, the analyst is able to hear only what he, potentially at least, is able to say."

2. Willard V. O. Quine, *Word and Object* (Cambridge: The M.I.T. Press, 1960), pp. 5-7.

CHAPTER 12

Recognizing Essentials

The distinction we are now to examine, between the essential and the adventitious, has, in contrast to many we have previously studied, a kind of invisibility. In this respect it is like the distinction between vague and distinct judgment. There is no particle, inflection, or arrangement in grammar or syntax to announce whether a particular statement is based on essentials or on coincidentals; nothing reveals this except the kinds of things the speaker says as his speech continues, and no symptom or warning can substitute for our own ability to discriminate between the essential and the accidental in the subject he is discussing. How this distinction comes to light is our present theme.[1]

We sometimes tell people things which seem to be redundant. It is usually tautological and uninformative to declare that a soporific puts one to sleep, or that teachers educate students. Redundancies are usually left unformulated because they do not need to be stated; they are what we take for granted when we speak. But sometimes the course of conversation moves in such a way that we sense the need to state a redundancy, to define what something is or what it does in itself. Strange things are said which seem to show that the speaker is ignorant of something he should take for granted. This is the kind of situation we must examine if we are to understand why we sometimes must say what a thing is, for only in such circumstances do definitions perform their proper work. If they are stated when uncalled for, they are indeed otiose; and if we carry out our philosophical analysis on lazy cases, we should not be surprised to find that definitions are pointless and that there are no such things as essences.

Imagine an invitation to participate in an academic discussion. Each person is to deliver a short paper. In describing what is desired, the invitation states that the papers should be about twenty minutes long, suitable for publication, adapted to such and such an audience, and serious, that is, based on the best information available. The first three attributes are informative and deserve to be mentioned, but there is something odd about mentioning the fourth. It is like saying, "Build a boat: fifteen feet long, white, wooden, and capable of floating on water." It is pointlessly redundant to mention that a boat is to float on water, or that a "real" academic paper is to be based on the best available information. It may on occasion be necessary to warn someone to make a good boat, or to write a good paper, and then such redundancies may not be pointless; but this is not the case in our two examples, because in them the redundancy is listed along with other attributes which are not redundant but informative. The speaker in each case seems to think he is telling us something new when he adds his fourth attribute; but if he thinks so, he does not know what a boat or an academic lecture is "in itself."

No one who understands English would make this kind of mistake about the boat. If we hear an error like this, we presume the man is not clear about the word he is using. But we can readily imagine, or even remember, examples of such misunderstandings about things like an academic lecture. A man may speak English perfectly well and not know that an academic lecture is to be based on the best information available. The fault lies not in poor vocabulary, but in his not knowing what an academic lecture is. He does not appreciate its essentials. Usually his ignorance of the thing will manifest itself in his inability to give a proper lecture himself, or in his inability to discriminate between a good lecture and a poor one. Sometimes, however, it becomes manifest in what he says about addresses, as in the example we have given.

By stating a redundancy as though it were informative, a speaker can embarrass himself and startle or amuse others; he suddenly discloses that he never did understand the subject of conversation.

His ignorance is exposed to those who know better—it remains
unregistered if the others are no better informed than he is—and at
such a moment the interlocutors are, almost always, at a loss as to
what to say next; the speaker who betrayed himself has also been
disqualified from saying much more and from being taken seriously, because his lack of appreciation of any single essential element calls into question his grasp of all the rest. The discussion, or
at least his engagement in it, is put out of gear. However, there was
a period before the disclosure during which the interlocutors may
not have known, or at least may not have been sure, that the speaker
was ignorant of what defines their subject. He may have made some
moves in the discussion which were reasonable enough. His blun-
der is not the first thing he says, nor is it contrasted to sheer silence
or to a whole series of erroneous statements, but to some plausible,
promising remarks; the mistake is conspicuous because it frustrates
an expectation that his earlier statements aroused. If he has said a
number of sensible things about the topic, we take it for granted
that he knows the essentials about it and are surprised when he
shows he does not.

How is such a deceptive impression made possible? How can
someone use words without knowing the essentials involved in
what he refers to? If the person speaks English tolerably well, he
will be able to use the term "academic lecture" as a name. This is
not just the result of studying dictionaries or having been told by
others what the words happen to mean; he has been around such
lectures, has experienced them, and can recognize a man lecturing
as opposed to a man painting a wall or a man playing a guitar. Such
naming and recognizing are based on his acquaintance with many
of the circumstances of a lecture: someone is before a lectern, there
is an audience, there is an academic topic advertised, it takes place
in an academic setting, the speech has a certain professorial style
and certain groups of words recur in it which are generally perceived as academic. The thing he knows is indeed, for him, a con-
geries of accidents, and his acquaintance with it allows him to use
certain names which he has associated with the accidents. But he
does not know what is going on; the names he uses "fall in" with
the object named just as coincidentally as the accidents that accompany it. There is no necessity in his naming. In this state of

mind—which is the condition all of us are in about some things, and some of us are in about many things, but practically nobody is in about everything—he does not know the essentials of what he recognizes.

He does not appreciate the adventitious either, since that is known only in contrast to the essential. He may realize that some aspects are not necessary; for example, the lights could be brighter or darker, or the speaker could talk more quickly or more slowly, without changing what is going on, but these are the accidentals of any kind of speech, not specifically the accidentals of an academic lecture. The adventitious and the necessary are confused with one another. In this confusion, the essential may be taken as adventitious (when someone says that the boat should float, or that the scholarly lecture should be based on serious materials), or the accidental may be taken as essential: certain clichés or certain flourishes may be considered to make the scholarly lecture what it is, the boat may be defined by a particular shape, a book by a particular color and size. An example of the former (a redundancy mentioned as if it were informative) is found in this press report of a veterans' meeting: "The comraderie between these veterans is stronger today than it was after each of the wars. . . . They are a breed of people that will some day become extinct—but not so until the last one of them is gone." And how shall we classify the violation of essentials in Edward Reep's remark, "Whatever his direction, Grosz was a brilliant draftsman whose limitations knew no boundaries"?[2] In a more general way, the chatter of Miss Bates in *Emma* and the remarks of Lydia in *Pride and Prejudice* both reveal an inability to distinguish essentials from the adventitious, a deficiency that proves harmless in the first case but disastrous in the second. Miss Bates carries on long speeches that move purely by association from one topic to the next, but she means well and usually helps others; but Lydia is light-headed in what she admires in people and things, and she marries a man whose attractive appearances conceal a dishonest and selfish personality. Some of Jane Austen's most interesting characters are those who cannot perceive, whether for a period of time or permanently, what is going on around them; the play of the clear and the obscure in the way things are registered is an important part in the action of her novels.

There are some things that practically everybody understands. Almost anyone who experiences a boat can see that the point of being a boat is to float, and that it is redundant to add that requirement when describing one. Hardly anyone fails to see that a house is a shelter, or that animals move around, react to things, feed themselves, are generated and reproduce themselves. But there are many other things for which it is hard to get the point and to distinguish between what they are and what they just happen to be. Many people can use words for things like politics, political office, citizenship, war, diplomacy, poetry, puritanism, violence, the past, or friendship and yet be unable to distinguish the essential from the adventitious. In a discussion of a campaign for political office, for example, items such as charm, looks, the appearance of friendliness, the impression of sincerity, or even friendship with the person speaking often emerge as the reason a particular candidate is judged worthy of election. Something like rhyme or lofty words may be taken to be what "makes" a poem, or erratic emotional behavior may be taken as what constitutes an artist. Simpleminded movies, for instance, often develop incidentals as essentials and hence caricature what they intend to portray. For every kind of object that requires some discrimination there are an unlimited number of incidentals that can be taken as essential, and they may even vary from one person to another, because they are determined not by what the thing is in itself but by associations the person happens to have in connection with the object. There are no limits to insubstantial thinking.

The distinction between essential and adventitious is often better recognized in the way people behave toward the things named than in the way they talk about them. To be experienced in a certain area is primarily to become familiar with the distinction as it occurs there and to act in accordance with it. A good auto mechanic will get to the essentials of a problem quickly, while an amateur will get involved with countless incidentals; a good doctor will know what to look for in response to certain symptoms, while a layman will worry about many things that have nothing to do with what ails him; a good organizer will be able to arrange things expeditiously, while someone confused about the issues will just move things around. In all such cases, skill is not merely the result of repeated experiences. The repetition must be accompanied by the power to get the point, to differentiate the essentials from what merely comes along with them. If this ability is lacking, the repetition will be of little avail.

This distinction ranges over whatever we can think about and whatever we can affect by our actions. It is not found just in concrete individual objects, like animals, houses, or boats. It occurs also in actions, processes, issues, the making of things, relationships, and in such imprecise realities as the past and future, history, justice, a baseball game, government, and ritual. If the distinction is at work in what we say and do, we speak and act intelligently in regard to our subject; if it is not at work, we are in the dark about what we do or discuss. Being in the dark does not mean never having encountered the object in question; it means we might be able to name and recognize it but are unsure about the difference between the redundant and the adventitious. The darkness may affect our behavior toward the object, or it may affect what we say about it. The obscurity is recognized as darkness—as oblivion of the difference—only by someone who is not in the dark about it. His response is to state a pointed redundancy, either positive or negative: a boat has to be able to float, a lecture should be based on good information, a poem does not have to have rhyme, a politician does not have to have good looks. The redundancy may be stated in response to someone's confused speech about the issue in question, or as a way of getting him to stop acting improperly and to begin acting appropriately in regard to it. And even though both sentences may look exactly alike, the pointed redundancy is quite different from the pointless one uttered by someone who thinks he is conveying information when he states it.

The distinction between the essential and the adventitious is recognized in four ways. (a) It first appears to someone who thinks and acts intelligently in regard to the area in question. Even if he cannot formulate the appropriate redundancies (he may think it idle when anyone does state them), the distinction becomes operative in what he says and does. This is the first acknowledgment of the difference, and all subsequent, reflective recognitions are based on this one. It is achieved not by a philosopher, but by someone engaged in responding to the things in question. (b) Once the distinction is established in this way, someone can begin to state the redundancies that express the essentials. This is a second kind of recognition; it can be done, for example, in something like an essay on diplomacy, war, or music. Such a statement is often called "philosophical"; it is a meditation on how things have to be; it mentions the necessities of things. The listeners or readers know the speaker or writer is not engaged in reacting to the objects, but that he has become reflective, pensive, disengaged. He makes thematic certain aspects of things that have asserted themselves in the earlier, nonreflective intercourse with them. A skilled diplomat, in carrying out his activities, would recognize the distinction in the area of diplomacy in the first way we have mentioned, while an essayist like Walter Lippmann or Vermont Royster would recognize it in the second way.

The essentials acknowledged in this second way are often expressed as the thoughtful element—as opposed to the structural design—in poetry. As Victor Shklovsky, one of the Russian Formalists, has said, the work of art should "make the stone *stony*."[3] The poem helps us sense the essential and the necessary in what it is about; every poem captures or illustrates some such necessity in what it says, and it comes through as the knowledge the poem enables us to possess. If it fails to register some such necessity, the poem seems anecdotal and merely "nice."

(c) On a third level of recognizing the distinction, someone may begin to talk formally about the difference between the essential and the contingent and show how it becomes disclosed to certain minds and concealed to others. The remarks from this perspective are not about the essentials of any particular kind of thing, but about the essential and the adventitious as such. In this chapter we have been occupied in such discourse. We are speaking of the same distinction that was recognized on the two earlier levels—by the engaged intelligent speaker or agent, and by the reflective essayist—but we recognize it in a new way. Our present recognition could never have taken place without the first two. It is most properly the philosophical analysis of the difference. What is done on this level can, however, also be expressed in certain kinds of poetry. Poets often write about disclosure as such, in contrast to writing about war, love, birth and death, or other things which are the materials disclosed. The theme of disclosure sometimes hovers around the ordinary, "mundane" themes and their necessities, but sometimes it becomes the predominant theme, in a work like *A Midsummer Night's Dream* or in the work of poets, like Wallace Stevens, who write about being a poet.

(d) To close this series, and to relate it to the levels of analysis discussed in the last chapter, we must mention a further perspective, the metaphilosophical, from which we can recognize the distinction: we can now identify and talk about the distinction between the essential and the adventitious as it is recognized on the third level, by philosophical analysis. On this fourth level too we can register further, highly formal necessities about the distinction.

These four ways of recognizing the distinction between essentials and accidentals are parallel to the four ways of employing prepositions—the naive, the reflective, the philosophical, and the metaphilosophical—which were described in the last chapter. And if we take the preposition as representing syntax or grammar generally, we can say that the four levels in the way we employ formal structures of linkage are parallel to the four levels of discriminating between essential and incidental in the "content" found with the formal structures. Furthermore, in each of these two sequences, the first level arises from a matrix. The distinct, explicit use of grammar and syntax emerges out of vagueness, and the first discrimination of essential and accidental by an intelligent agent or speaker comes forth from the dark oblivion, the river of forgetfulness, in which the distinction is unsensed. Both sources, vagueness and oblivion, are one and the same and give rise to inconsistency and incoherence. In each case the emergence of the first level out of the matrix is described and analyzed by someone who speaks from what we have classed as the third, or properly philosophical, level.

Philosophical studies of essence often spoil their analysis by not recognizing (1) that the distinction between essential and adventitious is not simply "there," but that it emerges from vagueness, obscurity, indistinctness, and oblivion in our speech and action; (2) that the essential must be played off against the accidental, and not taken as somehow available all by itself; (3) that the work of philosophy is to describe how the distinction emerges, what it is related and contrasted to, and to whom it becomes manifest. It often seems to be thought that the work of philosophy is to pick out essences, or to select which statements, among all those we utter, are redundant or analytic. Philosophy, in this conception, has a special eye for essences and can instruct the nonphilosophical person about them. Philosophy seems to elbow others out of the way, to claim it can inform them about what is necessary in the things they experience. But this is not philosophy's work; the man who is intelligent and experienced in a given domain is the one who recognizes what is essential and what is adventitious. His achievement is first and utterly irreplaceable. Philosophy thinks about a difference that has become manifest to him; it does not establish a difference he is unaware of.

If we take away the task of identifying essence, is philosophy left with anything to do? There is nothing left to do if one assumes that "doing something" is carrying out action, experience, and thought within the arts, the sciences, and in ordinary life; philosophy does not continue along this line. It neither corroborates nor conflicts with what is done by the arts, the sciences, and in ordinary life and action. They maintain their integrity against philosophy. But if thinking about the arts, the sciences, and ordinary experience, and about the differentiation between redundant and adventitious that takes place within them, can be admitted as "doing something," then philosophy still has something to do when it loses its putative role as custodian of the analytic.

The ability to distinguish essentials from accidentals is indispensable in two respects: no subsequent form of thinking, no philosophy, can ever substitute for it; and nothing can instill it in anyone. Schooling as such does not bestow the sense for the essential, although it may cultivate it. Some people may develop certain skills, even linguistic skills, and still be indistinct in dissociating things. It is neither possible nor necessary for everybody to have a sense for the essential in everything, but it is necessary, for the health of a community, that the disseminated opinions are in harmony with the essentials of things. In this regard, the opinions of prominent people or "gentlemen" are especially influential, so the character of the education they receive is important for the society in which they live. A school cannot confer the power to discriminate essentials, but it can convey right opinions about them, which, as Plato observed, can be as effective as insight in regard to public consequences (*Meno* 97-99). To respect the essentials of things is not only a matter of cognition and speech; if I behave in a way which contradicts the redundancies of such things as politics, religion, human desires, pleasure, food, money, even magnetism, gravity, or chemical substances, these things will damage me and perhaps those around me, even if I never try to define them in speech. Disseminated opinions which are true and relevant allow such things to be taken as they ought to be, and permit me to enjoy them as they should be enjoyed.

If someone does have the ability to discriminate between the essential and the adventitious, it will assert itself when he acquires, in his education and instruction, a sufficient arsenal of categories and distinctions. These are provided in the general and the specialized languages he learns: English, German, or French, for example, and the languages of law, politics, football, or medicine. The languages are not learned in isolation from activity, for many of the names require that the person learning them *do* something in order to perceive what is named. It is of course possible, as Plato warned, for instruction to fail of its purpose because of the ignorance or wickedness of the instructors, and then a man's sense of the essential may be confounded instead of being released (*Republic* 491-95, 560-61).

People often try to substitute criteria for the activity of distinguishing essentials and accidentals. An essay may be judged to be good because of the journal in which it is published; a painting or building is praised because it costs a lot of money; an achievement is deemed good because certain people say it is. The use of criteria is an evasion of the responsibility to think. We must rely on criteria in many areas because we cannot become expert in everything, but if we have any responsibility for making a judgment in a particular domain, if our evaluation and decision make a difference, we are obliged to know enough about the matter, and to take sufficient pains, to let the essentials of the issue assert themselves in our minds. In this regard, sometimes the criterion of the value of things becomes the amount of money people are willing to pay for it; such an emphasis on money as the measure of things leads to an alienation of thinking which is socially as serious and destructive as the alienation of labor. The necessities and excellences of things in themselves are not allowed to come forward, and the thinking, acting, and making which are the counterpart to such disclosure do not take place either: "Usura is a murrain, usura/blunteth the needle in the maid's hand/and stoppeth the spinner's cunning" (Ezra Pound, *Canto* XLV). The treatment of money in the *Republic* and in Book I of the *Politics* shows that this problem has not come into existence only since the Industrial Revolution, but it does become more acute in a commercial and industrialized society.

Every name involves some necessities, the unmentioned essentials that operate behind the things we explicitly say. Furthermore, there is a temporal aspect to the necessities belonging to the object named. If the object takes time to become itself, it is named in anticipation of what it is to be when it is most real and most itself. A human being is most himself when he is acting or thinking according to specifically human excellences, but we can still call an infant a man even though he cannot do such things yet; he is the kind of thing that is most itself when it is engaged in the essentials of human performance.[4] Likewise a boat being built cannot float yet, but the essentials of what it is inchoately involve floating. We could not name this arrangement of planks and bolts except by involving the term "boat" and its essentials in our name. Furthermore, just as we can name and define something according to what it will become when it is most itself, we can also name superannuated or deficient instances only by reference to what they should be or have been. Although a sunken boat does not float, it is still nameable as a boat, and an incapacitated or senile human being is still a man. Sometimes we add adjectives to indicate incomplete, declining, or deformed instances (a young man, an old horse, a leaky boat) and sometimes we have special words for things in these conditions (an adolescent, a nag, a hulk), but even in the latter case the essentials of what is named involve the essentials of the object in its proper condition. The essentials of the adolescent involve the essentials of a man; the former are defined in terms of the latter, and the name of the former includes this refraction of the latter.

There is an evaluative element in the understanding of names. To use the name of a thing properly involves knowing what it is for that thing to be itself, and it is itself most thoroughly when it is at its best. If we do not know what it is to be a good man or a good boat, we do not know the essentials of being either a man or a boat, and our use of these names is then guided by collections of the coincidentals that come with the objects. Our use of the name falls apart into the adventitious if we do not know the good appropriate to the name; awareness of the good pulls the coincidentals together and gives necessity to what we say about the thing we name.

The difference between simply being and being in an excellent condition is more conspicuous the more complex and varied the thing in question is; it is less obvious for stones and sand, more obvious for living things. The difference can become obliterated if we do not ask the right questions of each object, if we fail to be interested in the way the object works when it is most itself. This failure occurs systematically when we disregard function and examine only structure, and it occurs in an extreme way when we reduce the structure to its sheer mathematical units and relations. Even if the structure is analyzed diachronically, such a mathematization washes out any question of intrinsically better or worse states (that is, states that are said to be better or worse in regard to the object's own operations and not in respect to the use we can make of it); it also eliminates any consideration of imperfect, mature, and declining conditions. Statistical analyses of social structures and politics, purely formal analyses of language, purely structural analyses of myth, and the purely mathematical interpretations of nature all do this. The things in question still have their good and bad, imperfect and perfect states—disease is not health, a tyranny is not a monarchy, doggerel is not poetry, a child is not a man—but our method obfuscates these distinctions. The mathematizing of things bleaches them of their excellence the way money does when it is taken as the sole measure of what is valuable.[5] When this way of thinking prevails, it is not surprising that the essentials of things become dismissed as only ideological projections of someone's point of view, that names are taken nominalistically, and that the goodness attributed to things is explained away as the investment—financial or psychological—that we make in them.

If real names involve necessities and essentials, names which turn out to be unreal are thereby found to be empty of necessity and the essential. This happens, for example, in the names used in superstition, words like "witches" or "the evil eye" or a "lucky number." Such words are not used, by those who take them seriously, as fictional names; they are purported to name things that enter into the events we live through, while fictional objects are taken as discontinuous with our world. Further, they are believed to name substantial conjunctions. But if the belief is shown to be superstitious, the person who used the name is not shown to have named apparitions or fantasies of some sort; he may have named a conjunction between winning something and using his lucky number, but this conjunction is shown to be coincidental, "nothing" in the sense of no substantial togetherness, not "nothing" in the sense of an hallucination. He used an unreal name because he named a coincidence as though it were a substance. In fact, what he named falls apart into two or more things, each of which has its own essentials and necessities, but the conjunction has no cohesion beyond what he projects into it.

Just as distinct thinking has to be contrasted to the vague use of language and not to sheer silence, so the appreciation of essentials has to be contrasted to a consciousness inundated with accidentals, without the reliability and identity that the essentials of a thing provide. It is not to be contrasted to complete ignorance of the thing in question. Furthermore, our claim that we can recognize essentials in things is not a claim that we somehow have visions of essences, or that we just look inside ourselves or to some detached world to find the necessities of things. Recognition of essentials is embedded in experience, but it is more than a mere accumulation of experiences; it is thinking. It does not occur in the same degree to everyone, and we can most vividly see what the appreciation of essentials is when we sense what its absence is like in the things people say and do.

Notes

1. For an analysis of Husserl's treatment of this subject, see Robert Sokolowski, *Husserlian Meditations: How Words Present Things*

(Evanston: Northwestern University Press, 1974), chapter 3, "How To Intuit an Essence."

2. *The New Yorker*, December 16, 1974, p. 160; and September 29, 1975, p. 112.

3. "Art as Technique," in *Russian Formalist Criticism: Four Essays*, trans. L. T. Lemon and M. J. Reis (Lincoln: University of Nebraska Press, 1965), p. 12.

4. The sense of a thing's being itself more at one time than at another is implied in T. S. Eliot's remark, "It is by no means self-evident that human beings are most real when most violently excited. . . . " *After Strange Gods* (New York: Harcourt, Brace, 1934), p. 59.

5. See Robert Sokolowski, "Husserl's Protreptic," in *Life-World and Consciousness: Essays for Aron Gurwitsch*, ed. L. E. Embree (Evanston: Northwestern University Press, 1972), pp. 63-68.

CHAPTER 13

Philosophy: Analysis of the Kinds of Presentation

In discussing philosophical discourse, we must recapitulate some stages of speech that we have already examined. This not only will allow us to move logically into the philosophical dimension, but will permit us to show how philosophical identifications bring to completion the identifications and linkage achieved on the several prephilosophical levels.

(1) Let us imagine a gardener who says that a particular tree on an estate is diseased. Whether he registers or reports this, he is concerned with the tree, which he articulates as diseased.

(2) The gardener can make thematic the fact which he has registered or reported and make it ingredient in a new fact: "The bad weather has made the tree diseased." In doing this he names the fact he earlier articulated: he now takes as a whole the tree/diseased, that which he earlier distinguished and held together in its attributional parts. Two remarks are necessary. First, when he makes this move, the gardener does not cease to be concerned with the tree. He has not turned from the tree to a concept, proposition, or sentence. He has merely involved the tree/diseased in a more complex fact. Secondly, he has, nevertheless, made what we could call a "reflection" of a sort, because he now turns back to something he had earlier established in a registration or a report, namely the tree as diseased. He moves back over what he has achieved. If the earlier articulation had not been done, this further step would not be possible. But this reflection should not be confused with a

reflection on a proposition, or with a reflection on an "act" of registering or reporting, or with philosophical reflection. Indeed, because of the ambiguity of the term, it would be best to avoid the use of "reflection" altogether, since it is often used indiscriminately to cover many different kinds of turns.

When the gardener makes the tree/diseased thematic, he has introduced complexities into the way in which the tree is presented to him. The tree is not a bare particular; it involves more than the dimension of the "as presentable" or the play of presence and absence which has allowed it to be a named tree; it involves more than the simple, expectant presence that would be available, as a limit case, in the evocative use of names, in which we use the word only to hold the object in focus for our exploration and perception; it even involves more than the presence of the tree as having some indefinite attribute or other. The tree is presented to the gardener as having this character of being diseased. Because the same term, "this tree," could be used for all the presences we have mentioned, the gardener would tend to overlook these differences in the ways of being present. They would be of no concern to him anyway, because his work is to recognize the tree's trouble, to find its causes (to make the fact ingredient in other facts), and to do something about it. In all the transformations of the tree's presence, he remains concerned simply with the tree.

(3) The gardener has an apprentice. When he hears what the gardener says, he registers or reports the same facts with him. He does not ask questions. He too is concerned with the tree and its condition, and also overlooks the differences in presence which the gardener merely "sees through" without noticing. The apprentice, although he is an audience for the gardener, does not introduce any new "turns" or "reflections" not achieved by the gardener himself. However, as an audience he does introduce complexities; the words sounded by the gardener are heard and are also at work in the apprentice, and the tree being articulated by the gardener is the same tree seen and articulated by the apprentice, even though the latter is standing nine or ten feet away and looking at it from another angle. The gardener is aware of these differences in speech and perspective; if asked about them he would consider them so obvious that they do not need to be stated, and he would not see

what could be done with them, since they in no way change the fact that the tree is diseased, that this was caused by weather conditions, and that we can probably do nothing to repair the damage. None of these things are changed if we look at them from this perspective or from that, from the viewpoint of the gardener or from that of the apprentice.

(4) The owner of the estate is less compliant than the apprentice. He has found the gardener to be rather hasty in making claims, so when he is told of the tree's condition, he does not register or report along with the gardener but takes the fact merely as the gardener's opinion. He takes the fact as supposed, as proposed, and makes the propositional turn or reflection. He does not have the tree/diseased as his object, but rather the "tree/diseased." If told the apprentice also says the tree is in bad shape, he would probably dismiss this with the observation that the assistant never has any opinions of his own but merely echoes what the gardener says.

The owner is also concerned with the tree while he entertains the gardener's opinion, but with the tree as proposed by the gardener. He is not concerned with the tree as a bare particular, but with the tree/diseased, which has come forward as the "tree/diseased" of the gardener. Imagine that the owner examines the tree himself and finds it to be diseased. He registers or articulates the tree as so conditioned, and in doing this he verifies the gardener's proposition. At this point the quotation marks on "tree/diseased" fall off for the owner, and so does the gardener's special connection with the opinion: the fact becomes reported by the owner as a fact for everyone. The proposition or the opinion disappears as an opinion or proposition, the propositional turn is cancelled, and we all go back directly to the tree and its condition. However, the estate owner does not register the fact as he would if he had simply come upon the diseased tree by himself and noticed its condition; he registers it as confirming or saturating a report made by the gardener. This is a part of the new presence of the fact. Disquotation is not the same as an original statement, nor is it the same as a mere repetition, like that of the gardener's apprentice, which has never gone through the critical stage of quotation.

When the owner looks to see if the tree is diseased, he may find that the gardener is wrong. What the gardener said is not the case;

that "the tree is diseased" is only an opinion or proposition of the gardener, and, it turns out, an untrue one at that. This attempt at verification, instead of making the quotation marks vanish and the opinion disappear as a mere opinion, reinforces the quotes and rivets the opinion more thoroughly to the gardener. It is not a fact, *only* an opinion which he mistakenly proposed. When we henceforth mention the "tree/diseased" we are concerned with the tree *only* as it has been proposed by the gardener.

The owner of the estate is primarily concerned with his trees, buildings, crops, animals, and their condition, not directly with how they are presenced to people who talk about them. However, he must realize that there is a difference between the way things are and what people say they are; he knows he cannot just listen to what the gardener says, that he must on occasion look for himself, and that he may find the gardener to be mistaken. The apprentice, being inexperienced and a listless fellow to boot, hardly senses this difference; for him things are simply what they are said to be. But the owner does acknowledge and make use of the difference between fact and supposition, as well as other differences associated with it. However, he does not attempt to think systematically about it. If someone, perhaps a stranger to the estate, were to raise questions and push him to clarify the distinction, he would say that the gardener's opinions are somehow or other in the man's mind or in his head, probably in the way images are in one's mind when one is daydreaming, and that the disease is somehow in the tree and not in the mind. But he cannot go beyond such vague discriminations, and to manage his household well he does not have to. His rough distinctions are sufficient for the purposes at hand, even though they do not do justice to the activity of being truthful in itself. And the owner concerns himself still less with differences like those among the following: the tree as a continuous object; the tree as named; the tree as seen from different directions; (the tree as articulated) as supposed.

(5) Imagine that the household is expanded to include a grammarian or linguist, not one who merely knows the rules for speaking correctly but one who enjoys seeing the structures of language at work in speech and likes to point them out to others. He would notice the subject-predicate structure in what the gardener

says and would observe more complicated subordinations of phrases and modifiers as the gardener builds up complex statements on the basis of simple ones. He would examine the apprentice's repetition of the statements and the owner's quotation or paraphrase of them. For the linguist it would not matter who made the statement first, and it would make no difference whether the remark was being made as a registration, as a report, or as verification. If the linguist knew many languages he might try to discover not only the general structures of his mother tongue but the universal grammatical structures found in all languages. He would attempt to reach these structures by ever wider generalization and greater simplification of structures found in particular languages.

(6) A logician joins the company. His interest is in the laws of correct reasoning and the formation of propositions, as opposed to the rules of language. He and the linguist might quarrel about what each is supposed to do, for the linguist might claim that in reaching the laws of universal grammar he achieves a description of the laws of thought and thereby does the logician's work for him; the logician would answer that he studies the proposition and its structures of composition, while the linguist studies sentences and their patterns. The logician is correct, but since he does not move into the philosophical perspective, it is hardly likely that he will be able to explain clearly and consistently how the proposition differs from the sentence, and consequently how he differs from the grammarian. The situation would become still more clouded if a mathematician appeared and introduced sets and algebraic relationships and defied the logician to show how these things differ from the proposition. And the grammarian, logician, and mathematician would hardly speak with one voice if the estate owner were to ask their advice about the "speculative" questions that someone once put to him and that he was never able to resolve to his own satisfaction: in what way do we speak about the truth of statements, how do we distinguish between an opinion and a fact, and what is the distinction between a tree and its diseased state? The mathematician is concerned with relations and sets and not with statements, the grammarian studies sentences, and the logician examines propositions and arguments; the logician, who seems to be the man to answer the owner's question because he has a lot to say about truth, lives professionally in a propositional attitude but does

not think about the propositional turn and the verificational return.

(7) Imagine next that a philosopher arrives at the estate. In contrast to the linguist, the gardener, and the others, he does not seem to be expert in any one special area. He talks about the things all the others discuss and does not stake out a region from which they are excluded. He does not seem to be professionally different from them, and yet he is distinctive in being able to clarify, on occasion, some of the apparently simple but troublesome questions repeated by the owner of the estate: what do we mean when we say a remark is only an opinion, or that it is true, or that it is confirmed or denied by the facts? The philosopher is not distinguished by competence in any particular area; how is he differentiated from the others now crowding the estate?

He has a perspective which is new. The gardener is concerned with the tree. He is also concerned with the tree as diseased, when he incorporates this fact into further facts. The estate owner is concerned with the tree, the tree as diseased, and also with (the tree as diseased) as supposed; he makes the propositional turn when he takes the gardener's remarks as merely the gardener's opinion. The linguist is not concerned with the tree, or even with the tree as diseased, but with the words and sentences used in talking about these things: "tree," "the," "The tree is getting worse." The logician is concerned with (the tree as diseased) as supposed, and with structural elements and relations it can be involved with, but not with how the supposition is to "fit the facts." Now the philosopher is concerned with [(the tree as diseased) as supposed] as presenced. He is also concerned with [the tree as diseased] as presenced. He is also concerned with [the tree] as presenced. This dimension of the "as presenced" has been at work in the speech, thoughts, perceptions, and activities of the gardener, owner, apprentice, linguist, and logician, but none of them directed his concern to it. The philosopher does focus on it, and this gives him articulation and clarity over something they all take for granted; he can say things they all think to be quite familiar and obvious, although they are not easy to state; and he has this distinction without learning about any domain that is new and different from what is there under everyone's eyes.

The turn from the tree as diseased to (the tree as diseased) as supposed, is the propositional turn. It moves to opinion, proposition, proposal, judgment; it turns to meaning. The turn from the tree as diseased to [the tree as diseased] as presenced, is not the propositional turn; it does not turn to meanings, and philosophical analysis is not an analysis of meanings. It explores how things present themselves. Some of the things that present themselves are meanings, and therefore this:

[(the tree as diseased) as supposed] as presenced

is one of the concerns of the philosopher. But there are many things that present themselves which are not meanings, and so the following:

[the tree as diseased] as presenced

[the tree] as presenced

are also among the concerns of philosophy.

Because the philosopher has adopted this perspective, he can handle certain transformations and moves that seem hard to manage from the other viewpoints. For example, when the estate owner verifies that the tree is diseased, he confirms what he earlier entertained as the gardener's opinion. The registration of the tree as diseased is seen as filling or saturating the act that maintains (the tree as diseased) as supposed. But this is a difference in the presencing of the tree as diseased. It is a difference which concerns the philosopher and which is overlooked, though used, by those who are concerned with the tree and its health. When people try to handle this difference from a perspective which is not that of the philosopher, they invariably try to classify it as one of the differences they encounter in things: it is said to be like the difference between a man and his statue or picture, or that between two distinct things, or that between a model or blueprint and the object depicted in it, or that between a feeling and the object that provokes it, or that between a thing and the sound we call its name. Differences between kinds of presencing are reduced to differences that are found among the things and features which are presented.

The presencing of the tree as diseased is in turn based on the presencing of the tree, and it is a philosophical task to trace the emergence of registrations and registrands from perceptions and things perceived. Most of the distinctions in the present book, for example, are distinctions in the presencing of things: how things are nameable, determinable in predication, exclamable, supposable, expressible, takeable as. . . , registerable, and reportable. For example, our treatment of sentential grammar as signalling is an attempt to describe some structural elements involved in registration, supposition, and verification. Unless these analyses are seen as explorations in how things can be present and absent to us, their purpose and sense are misunderstood. The philosophical perspective is reached by a philosophical "reflection" or transcendental "turn," but this is a maneuver very different from the reflection on a proposition or meaning, different from the reflection on a sentence, and different from that reflection on an object which precedes predication and the distinction of attributes.

Once the philosophical viewpoint is reached, we can describe many more elements in the presencing of things. The spatial aspects and profiles of objects we perceive, their coordination with the kinesthesia of the perceiver, the special perceivability of the perceiver's own body, the contrasts among perception, forgetting, remembering, association, imagining, and anticipating, the dimension of other perceivers who perceive the same object I do but from other perspectives, the way I can and cannot be aware of what they are experiencing—all these issues become subjects of study as we explore the many ways in which things become manifest. We examine the imagined as presenced, the remembered as presenced, the associated as presenced. The domain of thoughtful speech is only one part of this world, even though it is a predominant part since philosophy itself is carried on in speech, and the other domains are accessible philosophically as involved in or leading toward articulation in discourse.

Furthermore, when we say philosophical analysis explores how things are presenced, we include, as we have implied, their manner of being absent as well as present. For example, the kind of spatial absence that permeates our experience of material objects, of which only one side is given at a time, must be mentioned in our description of perception, as well as the way parts of the object go from absence to presence and from presence to absence. The structure of reporting a fact as opposed to registering it must be explored, as one of the possibilities implied in registration itself; we must also describe the kind of absence that works in remembering, forgetting, imagining, interpreting signs, picturing, associating, and the like. These acts, and the manifestation correlated to each, all involve particular kinds of mixtures of presence and absence. In addition, part of the work of philosophy consists in showing how that which we experience as good and that which is disclosed as obligatory are manifested and concealed to the human agent.

Besides the transitions from simple presence to absence and vice versa, there is the special kind of emergence of something present not out of sheer absence but out of obscurity and confusion and vagueness, which is a peculiar kind of interference with presence. There is an appropriate obscurity for every kind of presence, just as there is an absence appropriate to it; the obscure, and the transition from the obscure to the clear and vice versa, must also be explored. In philosophy it is incumbent on us to become clear about confusion. Our description, for example, in chapter six, of the passive, indistinct use of speech as a matrix for distinct thinking is an instance of the philosophical investigation of the obscure; so is our treatment, in chapter three, of the associative use of sounds as a basis for names. The absent and the vague, therefore, are the two contraries against which presence is contrasted. All the distinctions surveyed in this paragraph are differences in the presencing of things, not differences in attributes, like redness or illness, which things might possess. Differences in presencing are the theme of philosophy. They are not the theme of particular sciences like biology or physics, for each particular science marks out a special kind of thing or a special kind of attribute as its exclusive domain of study, but takes for granted the presencing through which its own study is accomplished.

Because philosophical analysis is concerned explicitly with the presencing of things, it can introduce and handle distinctions and relationships that seem perplexing to other points of view. For example, the "predicational crease," the distinction and combination engendered in a perceived object when it is registered as having a certain characteristic ("This tree is diseased!"), is named and described by philosophy. Because we are sure of our perspective and concern, we are not tempted to see this crease as merely a linguistic distinction, nor are we inclined to postulate an unknown substantial something beneath a series of attributes; the crease is a structure in the way an object comes to be manifest, and the only way of explaining it is to describe the more elementary distinctions that lead up to it, like the object's being "taken as" this or that, to describe what we do to let the crease occur for us, to describe how the same crease can become absent (in reporting or, along another line, in obfuscation), and how it can be achieved over and over again in new repetitions, by the same registrar and by others as well. Likewise, we will not be tempted to try to explain the associative pull as a neurological or mechanical effect, but will accept it as one of the structural possibilities in presencing and describe its patterns. Also, we will take shifters (token reflexives or indexical signs) not merely as possible structural elements in a language, but as linguistic signs that function in establishing a context within which the speaker, his speech, and what he registers or reports are identified and manifest themselves.

Although the philosopher speaks from a new perspective, he uses the same words employed by the gardener, by the gardener's apprentice, and by the proprietor; he uses, for example, the noun "tree" even though he means the tree as presenced and not the tree simply. For this reason we tend to think philosophy talks about the same objects everyone else talks about, and in the same way; and we become perplexed when philosophers begin to use prepositions and other grammatical elements in ways that seem to run counter to ordinary usage.

The step into philosophy, into contemplating and speaking about the presenced as such, is not totally gratuitous. There is a sense in which prephilosophical discourse remains incomplete until this step is taken. Philosophy will not make anyone a better gardener or even a better proprietor or linguist, but all these individuals are aware implicitly of the presencing of what they speak about, and occasionally try to formulate something about it. They may, for example, try to discuss how language works in truthfulness, or how imagination or dreaming differs from perception, or how pictures differ from things. If they are not clearly aware that they are talking about the presencing of objects and not about objects simply, they will almost invariably end by postulating new, superfluous entities in their discussions. We will have sense data or images as copies of things, concepts or propositions as things in the mind, a picture theory of memory, acoustic images instead of sounds as the "real" words, and unknowable noumena as opposed to phenomena, all because the presencing of things is taken to be another thing itself. Being accustomed to talking about things, we are inclined to think we are adding a new thing, or at least a new quality to things, when we are led, on occasion, to notice the presence or absence or obscurity of things. To avoid these duplicating dilemmas, the move into philosophy must be performed deliberately and systematically, with clear awareness of how it differs from other viewpoints.

In discussing names in chapter four, we observed that the play of presence and absence, the form of "as presentable," is what changes an object into a named object; but the user of names does not make the presentability of the object thematic. The philosopher does, and that is why he can talk about what constitutes naming and nameability. When he does talk about this, he names it: the presentableness of things, which allowed them to be named in ordinary speech, itself becomes presenced and hence nameable. The play of presence and absence is applied to the original play of presence and absence. Presentation becomes presented and named, registration becomes registered and reported. This manifestation of manifesting occurs when we make the transcendental or philosophical turn. There is nothing mysterious about it, despite the paradoxical way it has to be formulated: it is simply thinking and speaking about how we name, and subsequently articulate and talk about, things. When we use the word "tree" in philosophical discourse or transcendentalese, we use it to name the tree in its presencing, in its being, which is equivalent to its being truthful.

But if naming in transcendentalese is made possible by an appropriate play of presence and absence, what is the absence which is to work as the foil for philosophical presence? In naming material objects we have the obvious alternative of spatial absence; in naming temporal things we have the temporal absence which occurs at the end of a perception, we have the onset of forgetfulness, and we have the special absence which occurs in remembering something instead of seeing it. The absence that works as a foil in philosophical naming is the unthematic, anonymous awareness we have of presencing before we turn to it philosophically. For example, the "perceptual field" is with us all the time as we perceive houses and cars, but it is there for us in a new way when we think directly about it philosophically. This slight and subtle shift between the field as exercised but overlooked and the field as made thematic is the play of presence and absence that allows us to use the name "perceptual field" in philosophical speech. Because the shift is so slight, it is hard to name something like the perceptual field, and most persons would probably take it just as the space that is around us at a given moment. A similar play of presence and absence allows us to use the name "the tree's presence," or even, correlatively, "perception of the tree," philosophically. Furthermore, this same shift between the anonymously experienced and the thematically focused is equivalent to a clarification of something that is obscure, because the initial uses of terms like presence, perception, and the name-able, by someone like the estate owner in our story, are an obscure and confused attempt at philosophy. And once things like the presentability of objects become named, it is possible to involve their names in grammatical linkage and to make philosophical assertions.

We have spoken of the move to a philosophical "perspective," but strictly speaking the new position is not one perspective among many. Perspectives exist in the prephilosophical experience of things, where objects look different to different viewpoints at different times. When we explore the very having of perspectives, the experience and presence of things, we speak from within an attitude where everything should appear the same to whoever is speaking: it is not a temporary or local condition that material objects should be perceptible only one side at a time, that what is experienced can be forgotten and remembered again, that a speech can be brought from vagueness to distinctness and that it can be quoted by others, that naming involves the play of presence and absence, that registration is contrasted to reporting. If these things were not so, there would be no presencing of things and no actuality of mind.

Finally, "the mind" is only properly appreciated from the philosophical attitude. The mind is the accumulation of presences that has been built up within one receiver of presences, one dative of manifestation; it is further the potentialities that this dative has for more presencings. The mind is both receptive and active; by it we take explicit positions when we register and report distinctly, but these activities presume that it has gone through a more passive history of perceived, remembered, and associated acceptances, which in turn involve initiatives of their own. The mind becomes actual in correlation to the presences that accumulate in and for it. Like "rain" or "thunder," "mind" is a gerundial noun; the verb "to mind" or the gerund "minding" expresses its nature as much as "raining" tells us what "rain" is; mind is not a substance independent of its activity. Nor is the mind identical with the self or with a human being, because minding, important as it is, is only one of the things we can do. We may try to make the mind a substance or a thing when we forget that the word "mind" is used most properly in the philosophical attitude and when we attempt to designate it as another of the objects we run into along with trees and houses; then we immediately run into paradoxes with things like "*a priori* forms of the mind," which are imagined to be like spectacles through which we see objects; or we try to identify the mind with the brain. Mind is properly named as the minding of things, the having of their presences as well as their absences, in all the complexities this involves; and unless the presences are clearly and appropriately named, that which enjoys them cannot come to its proper formulation either. The fact that we do talk about the mind in our prephilosophical discourse indicates that such speech is incomplete and destined for paradoxes and dilemmas until the turn to philosophy is made.[1]

Note

1. For an analysis of the kind of presencing that occurs in images, see Robert Sokolowski, "Picturing," *Review of Metaphysics*, 31(1977), pp. 3-28.

CHAPTER 14

First Philosophy: Analysis of Being as Being

There are many differences which are important when we think and act in the prephilosophical attitude but which lapse into indifference when we enter the philosophical attitude described in chapter thirteen. The only distinctions among objects that make a difference philosophically are those that express different kinds of presencing. For example, the differences between an oak, a willow, and an elm are important to the gardener and to the owner of an estate, but the formal way each of these presents itself is the same, so for the purpose of philosophical analysis we could use any one as our example. On the other hand, the presencing of the tree's condition and the presencing of a proposition of the tree's condition (its condition as supposed) are very much different and constitute an important philosophical distinction.

There are some differences in the material cores of things which are also philosophical differences because they involve distinctions in presentability. Human beings and trees, for example, are not just different kinds of material objects, but have different ways of being perceived when appreciated fully and properly. Among other things, human beings are perceived as having experiences, feelings, and attitudes which we as perceivers could never, literally, situate within our own sequence of experiences, feelings and attitudes; but trees are not presented with this dimension of an inner, conscious life. This difference between objects is such as to require different kinds of presentational performances in anyone who experiences the objects. There are elements in our activity of perceiving other people, like sympathy and mutual understanding, which do not function in our experience of trees. Because philosophy is concerned with

(x) as presenced,

only those elements are philosophical which make a difference in presentability and in what we must do to achieve presence. Examples of philosophically relevant differences include those between fact and proposition, object and attribute, essentials and coincidentals, the perceived and the remembered, what is seen from here and what is seen from there, expression and the exprimend, naming and perceiving, the continuous and the discrete, the logical and the mathematical, the living and the non-living, and plants, animals, and humans.

These and many other differences are registered from the philosophical perspective. It should be emphasized that the turn from ordinary objects, from willows and whales, to the various kinds of presencing in which they become identified as objects is not a generalization. It is a "turn" and involves a change in the direction of our interest. To become concerned with image and imaged, or name and naméd, for example, is not to discuss more features that belong to willows and whales, like their color, shape, and behavior; it is to turn to those forms of presencing through which we have willows and whales and other objects and all their attributes. Furthermore, it is not the case that an object is fully established for us by itself, and that it then enters, as a kind of afterthought, into various relations of presentation, like becoming named, pictured, remembered, and seen from this side and that. An object is constituted as object only as being paired or presented and absented in these various ways. An object acquires a special sense of its objectivity, for example, by being appreciated as the original of an image; it possesses another sense of objectivity by being appreciated as that which is remembered now but was seen earlier. To be an object is to be at the intersection of many such kinds of pairs of presencing; and the kinds of presencing themselves, the subject of philosophy, work to establish objects for us. Without them there would be no objects; they "underlie" the willow and the whale as objects, and we must turn away from whales and willows to focus on what imaging, naming, perceiving, registering, remembering, and the rest are. We do so when we make presencing our theme and enter into philosophy.

Philosophy as the analysis of presencing involves the description of the structures that make up each kind of presence and absence, and it involves contrasting the various forms of presencing with one another. In addition we might catalogue the presentational pairs and ask about the relationships among them: In what way can they be dependent upon one another? Can an exhaustive catalogue of the forms of presentation be achieved? Is it possible to provide a "transcendental deduction" of the forms of presentation, an analysis that shows a necessary order of structure and development among them? We leave these questions for the time being, but our very ability to examine the forms of presencing and to raise these issues suggests that the forms themselves are not the ultimate thing we can think about; taken both individually and as a totality, the forms of presencing depend upon other elements that are to be scrutinized in another kind of analysis.

For there is a further turn to still another perspective, the move into metaphilosophy or "first" philosophy; from this location many of the philosophical distinctions of presencing lapse into indifference, just as many prephilosophical differences become insignificant when we enter into philosophy. There are very few differences that need to be registered in this final, first philosophical perspective, and those that need to be acknowledged here "underlie" the philosophical distinctions, just as philosophical distinctions underlie the ordinary objects of our prephilosophical experience.

What do we make thematic from the standpoint of first philosophy? Philosophy examines

(x) as presenced;

it describes the various structures that make up different kinds of presentability. It describes the play of presence and absence appropriate to the kind of object in question (spatial object, something remembered, fact, supposition), and it describes how the identification of that thing occurs in the play of presence and absence peculiar to it. First philosophy, however, examines presentability as such. It does not examine the different ways in which something can be present and absent, it does not examine the different kinds of presentability, it studies the elements of presentability itself. All the different kinds of presentability—image and imaged, name and named, aspect and thing perceived—are structures which in turn presuppose certain other, most basic structures, those of presentability as such.

What are these structures or elements of presentability as such? They are sameness and otherness, motion and rest, presence and absence. These couples are examined from the perspective of first philosophy. They do arise in, and are not peculiar to, any one of the ways in which something is presentable; they are not confined, for example, to imaging or naming; they are elements of presentability as such. First philosophy makes presentability thematic in itself, and registers the distinctions between being the same and being other, being stable and being in motion, being present and being absent. We will use the term "couples" to name these three (sameness/otherness, rest/motion, presence/absence), and will restrict the term "pairs" to name the various kinds of presentational forms (name and named, image and imaged, slant and object). The three couples are the elements of presentability as such, while the various presentational pairs are the structures in and through which we have objects. The couples underlie the pairs, as the pairs underlie objects.

The move from examining specific kinds of presentability, like naming or imaging, to examining presentability as such, along with its triangle of couples, is not a generalization. The couples sameness-otherness, motion-rest, presence-absence are not general features of imaging, naming, supposing, remembering, perceiving, and the like. We have to turn away from these kinds of presentability into another direction; we have to turn away from philosophy to first philosophy. This turn is analogous to the turn we have to make from our prephilosophical experience of things to philosophy: in that case we turn from experiencing and analyzing willows and whales and begin to make thematic the structures of imaging, naming, remembering, and the like, the kinds of presentability through which we have willows and whales, the structures which underlie willows and whales. The turn into philosophy is not a generalization carried out upon willows and whales; to be a picture or to be pictured, to be a name or something named, are conditions that allow willows and whales to be themselves as objects. Analogously, to be the same or to be other, to be stable or moving, to be present or absent are not general features of imaging, remembering, or naming, nor are they general features of willows and whales; they are distinctions that underlie such kinds of presentability, and they underlie—twice removed—the objects constituted in presentations. They permit the presentations to occur, and also permit the objects to be identified in the presentations. Sameness and otherness, motion and rest, presence and absence have to be in order to allow the various kinds of presentability, and the objects established in them, to occur.

We have said that philosophy examines the various kinds of presentation that occur, while first philosophy examines presentability as such, which involves the couples of sameness and otherness, rest and motion, presence and absence. It would appear that we have given a special preference to the third of these couples, presence and absence; this couple is primarily involved in presentability, and seems to be the preferred theme of both philosophy and first philosophy.

We have developed our distinctions with an emphasis on presentability, but now that we have reached a kind of closure, it is possible to admit that either identifiability in differences or stability in change might have been chosen instead of presentability as our guiding theme. In fact we have made use of the other couples as we developed the kinds and structures of presentability. We could not speak of the imaged presentation of an object without saying that the *same* object is presented perceptually and in pictures or reflections, and that the motion from being imaged to being perceived, or vice versa, involves a permanence of what is given. Likewise, we could not speak of the many-slanted perceptual presence of an object without implying that a single object is identified in a manifold of different appearances, and that the fluidity of the appearances is coupled with the endurance of the object. Each kind of presentation involves its special kind of identity or sameness in differences, and its special kind of motion and rest. In each case there is a play of sameness and otherness and a play of stability and change, as well as a play of presence and absence. If we had taken identity as our dominant theme, therefore, we would have to involve rest and motion and also presence and absence in our analyses, and the choice of stability in changes would in its turn require mention of sameness and otherness, as well as of presence and absence. Finally, first philosophy, besides being conceived as the study of presentability as such, could have been defined as the examination of stability as such, or identifiability as such; in each case the same distinctions of sameness-otherness, motion-rest, and presence-absence would have to be made.

When we speak of presentability, we do not mean presence alone, but presence and absence taken as a couple. When we speak of identifiability, we do not mean sameness alone, but same and other taken as a couple; likewise stability does not mean rest alone, but rest and motion taken as a couple. Philosophy, as we have defined it, examines the various kinds of presentability, identifiability, and stability; it examines the various plays of presentability, identifiability, and stability, such as imaging, picturing, naming, perceiving, remembering, registering, and the like, each of which engages all three couples in its own particular way. First philosophy, however, does not examine such plays or kinds; it examines what allows the plays to take place: the couples themselves which enter into each play. First philosophy examines presence and absence just as presence and absence (and not in one of their plays or kinds); it examines presentability as such, or presentability as presentability. First philosophy examines the same and the other just as the same and the other; it examines identifiability as such, or identifiability as identifiability. First philosophy also examines rest and motion just as rest and motion; it examines stability as such, or stability as stability. In examining these things, it scrutinizes what underlies picturing, naming, registering, repetition, and all the other plays of presence and absence, rest and motion, sameness and otherness, which in turn underlie the objects of our straightforward experience, such as willows and whales. Topics like identity and difference, permanence and change, and presence and absence cannot be treated in the way we treat boats and cows, nor in the way we treat various ways of having boats and cows presented; they must be treated in a more elementary way, as more basic than either objects or the kinds of presentation; we come to them only through the double turn, first to philosophy, and then to first philosophy. And of course, even though sameness and otherness, motion and rest, and presence and absence are "prior" to the kinds of presentation and to willows and whales, they are never found separately, by themselves, no more than the form of picturing could ever be encountered by itself alone; this inseparability does not, however, mean that the three couples could be reduced to what they condition and allow, no more than the inseparability of picturing would mean that to be a picture is to be Whistler's mother.

What can actually be said about the three couples studied by first philosophy? Obviously all the kinds of things we say about ordinary objects cannot be stated here; nor can we speak as we do about images and the imaged, names and named, and the rest. We cannot even use the various kinds of presentation to develop the themes we have here, because what we examine underlies them. Even the grammar of first philosophy would have to be justified, since it is not clear what should, in this science, replace the structures of subject and predicate, noun and verb, and the like. Still, to say that the triangle of couples is to be distinguished, and to say that it underlies the other levels of analysis, is to say something; the very procedure of locating problems of identity or stability or presentation on this level, and not on the level of, say, percepts or signs or ordinary objects, is insightful, and is part of first philosophy. Even if little remains to be said directly about the triangle of couples, there are various ways of reaching back into the triangle from the subsequent levels of experience—we could approach identity, for example, from the point of view of association, or from anticipation, or from numbers, or from pictures—and each of these retrogressive moves gives us a new appreciation of what the basic couples are, and how they are prior to what follows them. Further, the many negations we make about the couples and their interaction are informative. And finally, it will be necessary to speak of the couples as themselves derived from something like the Indeterminate Dyad and the One.

In speaking of the couples, we have on occasion used the term "being." We have spoken of being the same and being other, being at rest and being in motion, being present and being absent. Must we not somehow add "being" to the triangle of couples studied by first philosophy? Certainly being cannot be said to begin at one of the levels of analysis subsequent to this one; it must have its place with these fundamental elements.

Being blends with the other couples in a special way. Motion and rest, for example, exclude one another, but both are being. However, being is not said of them separately. It is not the case that motion is being, and that in addition rest is being too. "Being" here is not like "blue," which is said individually of two blue eyes. Rather, being belongs to rest and motion specifically as taken together. Rest and motion penetrate what is, but they do so only as a pair, taken together. It is not the case, say, that one part of being is at rest and the other part is in motion, and so being is totally covered by rest and motion; rather rest-and-motion, or the couple rest/motion taken as a whole, blends with being. The two following items are not the same: (1) to take rest first and then to take motion (or even to take rest plus motion), and (2) to take rest and motion together, as one. Only what is done in (2) is equivalent to being. To emphasize this in schematic terms, we must differentiate between (1) taking one and one; (2) taking one and one together, as "one" on a higher level (i.e., as two, which is a new kind of one). There is a surcharge, a kind of capping in (2), a further dimension that has not yet arrived in (1). Only the togetherness of rest/motion is being; only when rest and motion are taken together can we equate them with being. Being is the "being taken together" of rest and motion (analogous to the completion that arises when we have not only "one and one," but "one-and-one taken together, i.e., two"). Only when rest and motion are taken together, only as a couple, can they be; rest cannot be by itself, nor can motion be by itself; to separate either of them would be to think abstractly. They can only be— together. And no particular being can be without involving them; being is the couple, rest/motion.

What we have said of rest and motion is true of sameness and otherness and absence and presence. The same can never be without otherness, and vice versa. As a couple, taken together, they pervade being, and being is this couple in its conjunction; no particular being could be without sameness and otherness. Likewise, being is the blend of presence and absence, neither of which can be by itself.

However, being is not just the togetherness found in each of the couples. As studied by first philosophy, the three couples are also taken together, as a "triangle," as we have expressed it. Being is also this togetherness, this unification. No one of the couples could be by itself (no more than any member of each couple might be by itself); however, the couples as such are not equivalent to one another: motion/rest is not sameness/otherness, nor is it presence/absence. Besides being couples, they must also be taken together. Once again there is need for a surcharge, a capping, the completion of being held together: not as something adventitious, but as that which establishes the elements that are held together. The being-together of rest/motion, sameness/otherness, presence/absence is prior to any of these couples—and to any member of each couple—taken separately. They belong together and they are together; no couple could be without being with the others.

There might be some discomfort in making being the togetherness or the wholeness of the basic couples. It seems not to be enough; we seem to make being *only* rest/motion, sameness/otherness, presence/absence taken together. But being taken together *is* something more than what belongs to the elements which are assembled. This surcharge is not nothing. In fact, it is more than any of the elements—whether a couple, or a member of a single couple—because the elements *are* only when together with one another. When we take the elements together, we do not add a kind of subjective form or assemblage to them; we recognize their togetherness, which is more basic to them than any element can be by itself, because they are treated abstractly when taken apart. It is more proper to say that we intervene, that we introduce a "subjective form," when we take one of the elements by itself, not when we acknowledge them as together. Furthermore, this being together of the elements is not accounted for by any of the couples themselves; it needs to be "added" to them, but only in the subtle way that "two" adds something to "one and one": not by adding still another "and one" to the series, but by completion and closure, by taking "one and one" as a whole, as "two."

But this still seems to reduce being somehow to the couples, or to the triangle of couples. Doesn't being also have the sense of being actual, of not being nothing, of facticity? Is this not more than being the togetherness of the three couples? Wouldn't we even have to devise a new couple, being/nonbeing, and add it to the three we already have?

This is probably the most discomforting suspicion of all. This sense of being, as facticity, as existing rather than not existing, is a special sense that arises only when we move to a stage beyond first philosophy. It is a legitimate dimension, but it should not be introduced now. On the levels of philosophy and first philosophy, being simply means the final necessity, the ultimate context or horizon, the most elementary issue that thoughtful analysis can lead us to. The final context, that which cannot be resolved into wholes or parts more ultimate than itself, is being: that which must finally be acknowledged as there, that which is the setting for all subsequent analysis. And what do we run into there? The most elementary couples, taken together as a whole; the triangle of rest/motion, sameness/otherness, presence/absence: not as elements that could somehow "be" each by themselves, but as elements that are only by being together. Being is not reducible to these couples, because none of them as such accounts for their being together, and hence for their being, since they can only be with one another.

We have said that first philosophy examines presentability as such, stability as such, identifiability as such. We can also say that first philosophy examines being as such, or being as being. All other ways of thinking delimit being and study it as restricted to one way of being or another. Among the natural sciences, for example, biology studies being as living, botany studies being as vegetative, physics studies being as material, psychology studies being as conscious and desiring. Furthermore, in what we have called philosophy, we examine being as picturable (as being a picture or as being pictured), being as nameable, being as perceivable or rememberable, being as supposable, and the like. In all such cases, whether in natural science or in philosophy, we narrow being to a certain aspect and examine only that aspect. We deliberately leave out other ways in which we can "take" being "as" this or that. In the formula that expresses the object of our knowledge, the "as" in "being as . . . " works to confine. Furthermore, in all such cases we concentrate on what follows the "as": living, picturable, material, proposed, quotable. We forget about being, the context and horizon out of which we have cut the part we study; we even dismiss, as not part of our professional interest, the activity of confinement expressed by the particle "as."

Now when we examine being as being, we make a move that is defined precisely in contrast to the confinements that lead to other ways of knowing. The first part of the phrase, "being as . . . ," leads us to expect a confinement of being, a restriction to a particular way of being, with its accompanying forgetfulness of what underlies the confinement. But then the end of the phrase, ". . . as being," is an annulment of what we expect. It does not even edge us over into a new, unexpected aspect of being different from what we anticipated; it throws us back on what we always leave behind when we think. In this move, the "as" annihilates itself; but unless it did so, unless it led us to expect a confinement and then disappointed us, there would be no turn of our minds to this subject, which cannot be approached except in this rebounding way. We are turned back to the setting for all our thinking, we turn back to being as being. Since the first part of the phrase, "being," is the final context for all confined thought, we are thrown back, or we turn back, to whatever is ultimate as the border for thought.

And what do we find there? Not trees or atoms, not pictures or memories or percepts, but that which underlies all such things: the couples of sameness and otherness, rest and motion, presence and absence: not as an assembled crowd, but as together as one.

Being, as the final setting for what we experience and think about, pervades all that is. As we have seen in chapter two, gerundial forms in languages are the appropriate expression for realities like the weather, moods, the time, and moral and natural necessities, which are not differentiated into agent and achievement or subject and feature. Such realities are continuous, are expressed as immediately surrounding and pervading our world and ourselves, are no one's responsibility but emerge anonymously and by themselves. Being has all these characteristics in a greater degree and in a different way. There do remain some differentiations among moods and weather states: sadness is not anger, getting chilly is not getting dark. When we use gerunds for such things we have taken steps toward the differentiation of features and the isolation of contexts. But being does not involve even these gerundial differences; it moves in the other direction and strains against exclusions. It can never name merely an absent context, but it includes all contexts, absent and present, when it is used to name. Nouns, with their pull toward reference and the naming of what is absent, can occur within "being," but "being" cannot be confined to being a noun. Likewise, manifestations, whether features or actions, are differentiated from one another and from that which is manifested in them; verbs pull toward a particular manifestation and toward registration; but being involves the past, the future, and the elsewhere, as well as what is here and now. Because being straddles both presence and absence taken together, it does not break down into nouns and verbs, with their respective tendencies toward absence and presence, but remains gerundial.

Being and its couples pervade both the various kinds of presentation, like naming and picturing, and the objects and attributes, like willow and green, presented in them. Being pervades the object of philosophy and the objects of ordinary experience, science, and the crafts, as well as the achievements and virtues of action. But to be aware of this pervasion, or even to describe it, is not to tell anyone anything new about picturing or naming, or about willows, colors, atoms, or virtues and vices. In fact, statements about it seem tautological and otiose: to be told that the same object is available in the differences of picture and perception, or that the same object is stably perceived while we move through the many aspects it presents, is not to be told anything particularly useful or new. It is to be told about what we most take for granted: so much so, that when we are told about it, we may wonder why anyone would bother to notice such things. And yet to express these root tautologies can be helpful in warding off confused versions of them, of which there are many in the opinions people have about things like truth and the way things are; and to become informed about the final boundaries of things is its own reward for anyone concerned with thinking about such matters. Everyone makes use of terms like "the same" and "different," and makes distinctions like that between "I saw it myself" and "I didn't see it but I still know." The basic couples are the warp and woof of our language and of our prelinguistic experience in memory, association, desire, frustration, and satisfaction. They also weave through and hold together poems, pieces of music, dances, and paintings, many of which are sheer compositions of identities and differences, motions and stabilities, and presences and absences achieved and enjoyed for their own sake. But to make use of same/other, moving/stable, present/absent in these varied ways and to think distinctly about these elements are two quite different enterprises; being and its triangle of couples cannot be thought about or clarified while we remain in the attitude, and follow the methods, appropriate to thinking about houses, willows and whales, colors and atoms, and to writing poems and deciding political issues.

In contrast to the all-pervasive sense of being we have described, there is a more limited sense that is sometimes confused with it: we may speak of being as that which makes judgments to be true, or as that which is real as opposed to the illusory or the mistaken, or even as the essential as opposed to the coincidental. In this restricted sense, being would be opposed to, and would not include, the propositional domain, the area of appearance or illusion, and the accidental. But such things, in some sense, do exist. The narrower sense of being is used properly on the level of philosophy, which examines the modes of presentation and needs a term to distinguish between what truly is and what only seems to be. On the level of first philosophy, however, where being as such is to be studied, the term "being" includes the proposed, the coincidental, and what just seems to be; Plato accounts for this inclusion by blending being with otherness. Although the lower levels of analysis, the prephilosophical and the philosophical, can recognize error and falsehood, only first philosophy can account for their possibility, because it alone examines being in a way broad enough to encompass them as being.

The pervasiveness of being extends through mind and consciousness. "Consciousness" is simply another name for the various kinds of presentation: we can speak of pictorial consciousness, linguistic, associative, imaginative, memorial consciousness, and the like, and we mean the same as pictorial, linguistic, associative, imaginative, and memorial presentations; the only difference is that with consciousness we emphasize the dative, the one to whom the presentation occurs. Mind, in turn, becomes actualized as an identity within the sequence of consciousness or presentations. Since being and its couples are what allow presentation to occur in its many pairs, being also allows consciousness and the mind to come about. Mind itself can only come to be because of sameness and otherness, presence and absence, rest and motion, taken together in being.

Thanks to Plato, we have become accustomed to blending being with sameness/otherness and rest/motion, but is it not awkward to include presence/absence as one of the fundamental couples with being as being? Being and its couples are prior to any receiver of presences and absences; if being as being is to include presence/absence, does it not require some sort of viewer of this couple, one who would then have to be "beyond" being?

On the level of being as being, the couple presence/absence does not require a dative of manifestation; rather, the couple is the condition for a receiver of presences, and for the identities established in the plays of presence and absence. Being has to be revealable, or presentable, or truthful, to permit a receiver of truth to be established. If presencing and absencing only occurred in conjunction with a dative of manifestation, then being would be truthful only on a condition and not in itself. Truthfulness would come only "late" to being, like its capacity to be pictured or to be remembered. True, we cannot imagine presence and absence without a dative, but we cannot imagine the other couples by themselves either; we always imagine them only as they are realized in some object like a willow or a whale. Nor could we even imagine picturing or naming as such; all we can do is imagine the picture of a house and the name of a river. Presence/absence, or presentability, belongs to being as being. Furthermore, Plato does not exclude a couple like presence and absence from blending with being as such; he admits that the same and other, and rest and motion, may not be all the "highest forms" (*Sophist* 254C). The very fact that Theaetetus and the Stranger are able to examine the blending of these forms, and to take them one after the other, and to talk about them even with the adjusted grammar and transformed prepositions which such a theme demands, indicates that being as being and its primary forms do lend themselves to speech, with its parading of presences and absences. Sameness and otherness, rest and motion alone would not account for this.

It is interesting that Aristotle does acknowledge that presentability belongs to the final sense of being, but he also demands a dative for this presencing: he must postulate a thought that thinks only itself, in solitude and in ignorance of the rest of being, as the highest instance of being as being. In doing this Aristotle also reflects his disagreement with Plato as to what can be asserted as ultimate: the cosmos and the self-thinking thought are final for Aristotle, they are being in its ultimate instances. But for Plato being as such is resolved into something beyond being, the Good or the One and the Indeterminate Dyad. Some of Aristotle's sharpest metaphysical criticisms of Plato are directed to the necessity of this step beyond being, an issue to which we must now turn.

CHAPTER 15

Thinking beyond Philosophy

Being as being is the final setting for experience and thinking, because it involves the three couples which permit the identifications and dissociations which stabilize experience and thought and allow them to be carried on, by letting things appear out of obscurity. Being as being is the theme of first philosophy. But can questions be raised and can anything be said concerning what is beyond being as being? Are any moves possible beyond the blending of the triangle of couples: presence/absence, sameness/otherness, rest/ motion? Is being as being, the final and all-pervasive context for what we experience and think, in any way itself derivative? The fact that there are three couples with being as being suggests that a move beyond can be made, but this is a move beyond philosophy and first philosophy; what is talked about is no longer subordinated to the three couples of rest and motion, presence and absence, sameness and otherness, and what is said must be accordingly adjusted.

Following the lead of Plato and the Platonists, we can call what remains beyond being as being the Indeterminate Dyad and the One.[1] These are what permit the forms, even the couples or highest forms, to be blended with one another and with being. They permit togetherness (as being as being permits presentability, identifiability, stability): they permit the being-together of the triangle of all three couples and also the subsequent togetherness of each couple—for example, the play of presence and absence in its many varied kinds: the pairedness of image and imaged, name and named, fact and proposal, and so on. All these are participations in the Indeterminate Dyad and in the One. The Indeterminate Dyad itself is the very possibility of being related; as Aristotle says in criticism, Plato would have it that relatedness, "to be *with* something" or "to be *at* something" (*to pros ti*), is more fundamental than being a being (*ousia*) and constitutes the power that lets beings be (*Metaphysics* XIV 2, 1089b18; cf. 1088a15-b13, 1089b4-20). The Indeterminate Dyad cannot be reduced to or derived from the One, because it does what the One cannot do. The dyadic divergence is always there, and it is even prior to being as being; it permits those blends in being which, in turn, allow the further plays of presence and absence, sameness and otherness, rest and motion, to bring forth things like willows and whales as we experience and think them.

Being and its blended forms participate in the One and in the Indeterminate Dyad. Consider a single couple, like rest and motion: the couple itself, when taken as different and as two, participates in the Indeterminate Dyad; but when taken as the couple together, it participates in the One. Each member of the couple, the rest and the motion, is what it is only by *being with* the other; and this being with the other is a completion that is not achieved by either member itself; it is the participation of the couple in the One. A similar achievement occurs in the whole triangle of couples, which is another participation in the Indeterminate Dyad; the triangle of couples also participates in the One by its being together, by being one triangle and not one couple plus another couple plus another couple. Besides "one couple plus another couple plus another couple," all must be taken together as one three or as *the* triangle, all must be achieved as together, as one; and only as so taken can they be. No member of any couple, and no single couple, could ever be by itself; they *are* only by blending with one another, and the achievement of this blending is their participation in the One. Nor do the couples or their members come first, then to be assembled and collected into being together; they *are* only by being together, and any consideration of them apart is abstraction. Thus being and its couples reflect the strength of the One and of the Indeterminate Dyad.

On the next level, that of the various kinds of presentability—the theme of what we have called philosophy—there are subsequent participations in the Indeterminate Dyad and in the One. Here we have pairs: indicator and indicated, picture and pictured, name and named, perceptual slant and perceived body, predicate and subject, report and registration, supposition and fact. We have things paired in different ways, and each pair participates, in its own way, in the Indeterminate Dyad. But each pair is not simply one plus one; each pair is unified in its special way and taken as one. In each pair, each member is what it is only by being taken together with the other member. A fact is a fact only by being contrasted with a supposition, and vice versa. Each pair in these varied kinds of presentation therefore also participates in the One. Of course each pair also participates in being as being and in its triangle of couples: picture/pictured or supposing/stating, for example, each participate as a pair in presence/absence, sameness/otherness, rest/motion; each is a play of all three couples. For instance, Napoleon's being the same in his portrait and in his original presence can be taken as a participation in sameness and otherness, and it is easy to see how presence and absence are also at work here. But besides participating in the three couples associated with being as such, picturing also participates in the Indeterminate Dyad and in the One, because it involves the strain between picture and pictured, as well as the unity of the two as the single whole of picturing.

There is a participation in the Indeterminate Dyad and in the One on still another level, that which is examined not by philosophy but by ordinary experience and by mathematics. There we encounter ordinary things, trees and houses; but we also encounter groups of things, and in particular we encounter things taken in two's and three's and in other numbers. As Plato has observed, being two belongs to Hippias and Socrates in a way different from other features like being human, being courageous, being white, and so on.[2] Such features belong both to Hippias and to Socrates, each taken separately, as well as to both taken together; but two does not belong to each of them separately, it only belongs to them when they are taken together. Furthermore, it does not belong to them when they are taken merely one with the other, but only when both are taken together as one. *Two*, as *one* number, is therefore a participation in the One as well as a participation in the Indeterminate Dyad, since it becomes itself only by achieving the unity of things that are otherwise distinct from one another, and that serve as units in the number two.

It is legitimate to distinguish the number two and all other numbers from the pairs we find in the various kinds of presentation which philosophy studies, pairs like image and imaged, name and named, because the latter involve a radical difference in kind in the members of the pairs (the image cannot be the original), whereas in the number two both units are taken as equal in respect to their being counted. Here we have no original *versus* copy; as counted and summed up, both units are exactly the same in kind, and even their positions in the order of being counted could be reversed without damage to the one resultant number. Another reason for distinguishing between numbers and the kinds of presentation is that we must adopt different viewpoints when we explore numbers and when we explore the various kinds of presentation. To explore the characteristics of numbers, to determine their features (for example, being odd and even) and their relationships to one another, requires something less of a reflection or turn than we need to study the characteristics of naming or of imaging. Some turn from things to numbers is needed when we do mathematics, but it is not the same kind as the turn toward the forms of presentation. Still less is it like the further turn toward being as being and its couples, the forms of the forms of presentation.

The number two, the presentational pairs of image and imaged, supposition and fact, name and named, and so on, each of the three couples, and the blending of the three couples with being, are all participations in the One and in the Indeterminate Dyad. Each of these, in its own way, achieves the unification of different elements that by themselves do not account for their unity. The One and the Indeterminate Dyad run through each of these levels and forms and stitch them together. They also run through the philosophical and the first-philosophical reflections or turns on such levels and forms, and hold all of them together with each other too. Each unification, moreover, should not be thought as a static frame under which the joined elements are yoked; it is more like an occurrence or an achievement, like two things being unified when taken as two, or like a painting at work being a picture. The unification, the participation in the One, is energetic. The One itself is energetic: it is not a finished something which merely manifests itself in its many participants; it is the power of unification. Even being as being, as the togetherness of the three basic couples, is a reflection of the strength of the One.

The many participations in the One are not achieved separately from one another. For example, in appreciating a picture, we have the unification of many slants in a single perceived thing, which in turn is at one with its original in a pictorial way when that perceived thing is taken as a picture; and all this in turn involves the continuous oneness of the dative of manifestation, the viewer of the picture. Through these perceptual, pictorial, and personal participations in the One, there is also an appropriate participation in presence and absence, sameness and otherness, rest and motion; being as the togetherness of these three couples is also at work in the picture and the viewer. The One and the Indeterminate Dyad do their work all at once in this picturing and in all these other achievements, which do not occur separately but as one.[3]

Is it necessary to move beyond being as being to reach the Indeterminate Dyad and the One? Would it not be possible, and would it not be simpler, to locate the final dyad and unity in being as being? Could we, for example, equate the ultimate origin of differences in otherness and the ultimate source of unity in sameness, instead of moving into a dimension beyond being as being and its couples?[4] This would not suffice; it would imply that plurality arises because things are different from or other than each other; but otherness and difference are made possible only by the Indeterminate Dyad and the space that it opens up. Things are other than or different from one another upon a condition, and the name we give to this ultimate divergence is the Indeterminate Dyad. And things can be the same as other things, or even enjoy an identity with themselves, only upon a condition, and the name we give to this ultimate strength of unity is the One. The One and the Indeterminate Dyad allow things to be the same and to be other than something else. To illustrate this in the case of the number two, sameness would not suffice to cap this unit and that unit into being taken as a whole, as two: it is not insofar as this and that are in any sense the same that they are taken as two, but insofar as they remain different and yet are unified as a single two. Likewise, the sameness between picture and pictured arises upon the condition that the two are taken as one, in the activity of picturing; the unification of picturing—the participation in the One—is a condition for seeing the pictured as the same as the original. We do not see things as pictures because we see resemblances (sameness) between one and the other; rather, we see sameness because we appreciate something as a picture. The picturing play of participation in the One and in the Indeterminate Dyad is prior to the play of sameness and otherness. Further, single words are never achieved as similar or dissimilar to other words, except as set within the syntactical relationships that both differentiate and bind them to one another. The play of unification and divergence which occurs in syntax is a condition for words' being the same as or different from one another. Finally, even in phonemes the binary opposition is prior and allows one phoneme to be taken as the same as or as different from another. Togetherness and divergence are not consequent upon sameness and difference. Instead, by letting things be distinguished and yet held together as one, they condition and allow anything to be recognized as resembling something else or as different from it. The capacity of two to be taken together as one constitutes the space within which sameness and otherness, rest and motion, and presence and absence occur.[5]

Participation in the One is also the Good for whatever instance is at issue. There are degrees in the intensity of oneness that can be achieved: one picture can be better than another when the image and the original are more intimately together; a speech is more truly speech when what is spoken is more intensely there in the discourse; a city is more a city and a living thing is more an instance of its species when each is most at one with itself in its being and work. The unification which participation in the One achieves must always master elements which participate in the Indeterminate Dyad and, as such, strain against being one even though they become themselves most fully when they do become fulfilled by sharing in the One. Bones and flesh go their own chemical way and bring about the death of the organism; images, because they are not the original, become shattered or decompose, or attract attention to themselves as objects and hence disturb the presence of the original in them; passions can ruin a human being and factions destroy a city; speech becomes noise and no longer expresses anything, opinions are separated from facts and forced on other minds, one aspect of a thing is taken for the whole. The goodness of each thing is its participation in the One, but such participation has to be achieved against the strain of the Dyad. Slight as it might be, there is a resistance to be overcome even in counting two different things as a single two, because the differences in each individual—all except the numerical difference—must be cancelled and each of the individuals must be taken as equal to the other for the sake of counting.

Someone who develops an eye for the One and the Good in particular instances may, as Diotima tells Socrates, also get a sense of the Beauty in which they all take part, the One or the Good in itself; this is the origin which has no slants, no pictures of itself, no aspects under which it looks different or bad in any way; it does not itself share in the strain of the Indeterminate Dyad. But even this origin is sensed on the margin of the many participations of it that have come to be appreciated. This origin must not be thought as a thing, but as an occurrence that ultimately allows things to be. It is an awakening or a shining which occurs everywhere in all its participations, but continually recedes from view as the things which it permits to be attract our attention.[6] To have a sense for this occurrence is to move past even the final context of being as being, with its couples of presence/absence, sameness/otherness, and rest/motion, so it is to have an inkling of what happens before such fundamental differences come about. One of the ways of talking about the One and its work—which are not two, agent and action, but one at work—is by appropriate denials of the three basic couples. The way the One is "with" and "in" the play of presence and absence that occurs in picturing, for example, is not subject to the identifications or differentiations or the presences and absences we run into when we speak of a car being "in" the garage or "with" a trailer. Even the relationship between (a) the being together of picture and original (their participation in the One) and (b) the picture and the original as distinct entities cannot be articulated with the notions of sameness which we use in more common cases, such as in saying that this color is the same as that color. We are not speechless when we approach the One and begin to talk about participation, but our speech must be thoroughly adjusted; we turn from the experience of things to philosophy, we turn from the philosophical to first philosophy, and then we turn from all these to appreciation of the One—which cannot be appreciated without thinking of the Indeterminate Dyad as well.

The Indeterminate Dyad is irresolvable into the One. However, according to Thomas Aquinas, there is a movement of a different sort beyond being as being. With the world taken as created, Aquinas thinks of the turn beyond being as being as a move toward the unlimited act of *esse subsistens*. This act of *esse subsistens* is not set in tension with the necessity of the Indeterminate Dyad, the compulsion of divergence. It is meaningful to say that the one pure act of *esse subsistens* could "be" all alone (it is not meaningful to say that the Platonic One could "be" all alone). The contrast to *esse subsistens* is not differentiation, but nothing other at all. That there is, in fact, anything other than the one pure act of *esse subsistens* is due not to the necessity of being coupled and paired, the work of the Indeterminate Dyad, but to the unnecessitated choice exercised by the creator.[7]

This creative choice filters through created being and all the subsequent levels of presentability and things. It does not change the structures that are found on these various levels, but it sheds a different light on them and modifies how they are to be taken. Augustine, for example, takes necessary truths and numerical relations as illuminated from an eternal source, and Aquinas says that the divine light allows us to appreciate the truth of things. Things themselves are now considered as having *esse*, and all the perfections of each thing are given to it through *esse*, since *esse* is conceived by Aquinas as the perfection of all perfections and the actuality of all acts. The proper effect of God's power is to give *esse*, and so God must be with whatever is: *Quandiu igitur res habet esse, tandiu oportet quod Deus adsit ei, secundum modum quo esse habet. Esse autem est illud quod est magis intimum cuilibet et profundius omnibus inest* ("Therefore as long as a thing has *esse*, so long must God be present to it, according to the mode in which it has *esse*. But *esse* is that which is most intimate to each thing and most profoundly present in all") (*Summa Theologiae I.8.1*). Finally, because all things, including the speaker himself, are taken as being not through a necessity of divergence but through liberality, all beings, and the speaker himself, are considered as transparent to their creator; hence the form of discourse adopted by Augustine in the *Confessions,* a form which is addressive and not referential, is the appropriate form of speech for approaching what is first and last.

Notes

1. My use of this Platonic theme in the present chapter was prompted by the essay of Hans-Georg Gadamer, "Platons ungeschriebene Dialektik," in *Kleine Schriften III. Idee und Sprache* (Tübingen: Mohr, 1972); see also "Plato und Heidegger," in *Der Idealismus und seine Gegenwart,* Festschrift for Werner Marx, ed. U. Guzzoni, B. Rang, and L. Siep (Hamburg: Meiner, 1976). See my essay "Ontological Possibilities in Phenomenology: The Dyad and the One," *Review of Metaphysics,* 29 (1976), pp. 691-701.

2. *Hippias Major* (300-301); see Gadamer, "Platons ungeschriebene Dialektik," pp. 33-34.

3. What Heidegger calls *Ereignis* is also that which lets beings be (i.e., that which permits being as being); see *Zur Sache des Denkens* (Tübingen: Niemeyer, 1969), pp. 20-25. This issue is also the theme of Husserl's writings on inner time-consciousness; see Robert Sokolowski, *Husserlian Meditations: How Words Present Things* (Evanston: Northwestern University Press, 1974), chapter 6, "The Inside of Time."

4. Jacob Klein does this in his interpretation of the Indeterminate Dyad; see *Greek Mathematical Thought and the Origin of Algebra,* trans. E. Brann (Cambridge: The M.I.T. Press, 1968), pp. 96-98. If the Indeterminate Dyad is to be reduced to otherness, then the One would have to be reduced to sameness, and being would be prior to the One.

5. Although we have used the terms "Indeterminate Dyad" and "One" in this chapter, our usage is not meant to be a strict commentary on Plato. There may be differences between what we say and what Plato said, in particular concerning the connection Plato seems to draw between the Indeterminate Dyad and the Great and the Small; he seems to permit some kind of identification of the Indeterminate Dyad with matter or space or extension. The Indeterminate Dyad as we interpret it ranges over the presentational pairs of name and named, image and imaged, proposal and fact, and so on, as well as over numbers and magnitudes and things; would this

be permitted by what Plato understands the Indeterminate Dyad to be? Does he understand space or extension as something that "opens" the way to permit the presentational pairs to come about? (He certainly would not take space or extension in a Cartesian, mindless sense.) The issue is one for commentators to decide. Instead of using the term "Indeterminate Dyad," we might have used a formal expression like "a plus b" or "a with b" to name the divergence that is perpetually played off against the One, but this would have made it appear that what we talk about had less continuity with Platonic themes than it does. On "space" as involved with what permits being as being, see Heidegger, *Zur Sache des Denkens*, p. 24: "Insofern Zeit sowohl wie Sein als Gabe des Ereignens nur aus diesem her zu denken sind, muss entsprechend auch das Verhältnis des Raumes zum Ereignis bedacht werden."

6. See Heidegger, *Zur Sache des Denkens*, p. 23: "Der Entzug [muss] zum Eigentümlichen des Ereignisses gehören."

7. *Esse subsistens* must not be confused with being as being. Hegel attempts to analyze *esse subsistens* (or perhaps something like the One) on the level of being as being when he involves it with presence and absence; this is why he is forced to include rest and motion and sameness and otherness in his conception of God. Process theologians do the same.

Index

Absence: and desire, 3-4, 25; of context, 14-17; and association, 24; and deprivation, 26; and names, 28-29, 39; involved in presencing, 151; appropriate to philosophy, 154-55. See also Presence-absence

Accidentals: as a basis for names, 132; replace essentials, 133

Action: and speech, 16, 37-38; and association, 24; and essentials, 134, 139

Addressee: and reference, xvi-xvii; and names, 5-6; and syntax, 48-49. See also Listener; Speaker

Appearance, and being, 12, 169

Aquinas, Thomas, 62, 179

Aristotle: xviii; on verbs, 12; on voice, 25; on rhetoric, 48; on concepts, 62; use of prepositions, 127; on money, 140; on self-thinking thought, 171; criticizes Plato, 173

Articulation and assent, in propositions, 59

Association: and names, 3, 23-24, 36; and pleasure-pain, 24; replaces thought, 82-83; and thinking, 85; and vagueness, 97; and accidentals, 134

Augustine, St. 179-80

Austen, Jane 133

Babbling, and phonemes, 67-68, 70

Basic combination, in predication, 45, 47

Beauty, and the One, 178

Being: and thinking, xv; as gerundial, 21, 167; as measuring propositions, 107; and couples of presence-absence, etc., 164-65; as facticity, 166; as final

context, 166-68, 172; and first philosophy, 166; and various sciences, 167; has no exclusions, 168; as the true and essential, 169; includes the apparent and illusory, 169; not equivalent to the One, 176

Binary opposition, 69-70

Body, and speech, 92

Boswell, James, 86

Child's experience of presence-absence, 25-26

Chinese prepositions, 22

Choice, and propositional elements, 88-90, 101

Christianity, 21

Coherence: and lexicon, 10-11; of propositions, 77-78

Confirmation, of statements, 110

Consciousness, and kinds of presence, 169

Consistency: and syntax, 10; and propositions, 74, 77

Consonants: and writing, 66; and vowels, 66-67; and identity, 67-68

Contact words, 117

Context: 12-17; involves speaker, 13; and nouns, 13, 37; creating new ones, 17, 39; as variable, 68; for propositions, 75-76; of being, 166, 168, 172

Continuous beings, and gerundials, 20

Cores, of propositions, 77

Correspondence theory of truth, 111

Couples of same-other, etc.: 160; condition the kinds of presence, 161; involve two taken as one, 162, studied

183